.NET 9 for Web Developers

From console apps to production-ready web APIs and desktop clients using ASP.NET Core, Entity Framework Core, and MVVM

Labio Cruz

Published by: GitforGits

Publisher: Sonal Dhandre

www.gitforgits.com

Printed in India

First Printing: November 2025

ISBN: 978-93-49174-01-6

Cover Design by: Kitten Publishing

Disclaimer:

This book, including all its text, diagrams, and illustrations, is an original work developed for educational and informational purposes. The content is not affiliated with, endorsed by, or sponsored by Microsoft or any other company, brand, or entity referenced within. All brand names, product names, and trademarks mentioned are the property of their respective owners and are used in a descriptive, educational context only. Every effort has been made to ensure that no copyrighted or trademarked material has been copied or misused in this book. All diagrams and illustrations that are not original have been used with proper attribution and credit to their respective sources.

If you believe that any content in this book infringes upon your copyright or trademark, please contact us immediately at support@gitforgits.com. Upon notification, corrective action will be taken promptly.

Prologue

When I started working with .NET, I didn't start with code. I started with a problem that wouldn't go away. At the start of my career, I was responsible for maintaining an application that seemed to break in new and surprising ways every week. At the time, I didn't know a lot about software frameworks, and the depth of the .NET ecosystem was pretty intimidating. It was late when I first opened a C# file and started to explore. The syntax was sharp, the libraries were powerful, and the way .NET handled memory and structure felt like learning a new dialect of a language I already loved. With every line, I realized how much potential the .NET platform had. I wanted to not only fix problems, but also design software that could predict and prevent them. I wanted it to be strong, easy to test, and simple to understand.

I still remember my first experience building a console application. There wasn't a fancy user interface, just input and output, but you could see every success right away and every mistake was obvious. That simple app was just a to-do list, but it taught me a lot. Each task I added and removed reflected a real change in state, and it became clear that the code could be as dynamic as the people who used it. I was able to debug my own logic, watch how the flow moved through conditions and loops, and develop a sense of confidence and curiosity. The idea that every piece of software, no matter how big, could be understood by breaking it into these basic parts guided my learning from then on.

While getting more into .NET, I found the elegance of web APIs and the power of decoupling code through dependency injection. The move from console apps to service-oriented design felt natural and almost unavoidable. I saw how .NET made it possible to build systems that could grow, scale, and remain maintainable long after their first release. Integrating databases with Entity Framework, mapping data models, and enforcing business rules taught me that every solid application starts with thoughtful architecture. All the mistakes I made in the first part of my software development career, like hard-coded values, sprawling classes, and tangled dependencies, suddenly they all became lessons that shaped my approach to design.

And then the world of desktop clients called to my attention. The combination of XAML and C# in WPF created new ways to interact with data, and the MVVM pattern made complex user experiences clearer. The process of connecting a WPF client to a live Web API, handling real-time updates, and managing state was challenging, but rewarding. Each obstacle made it clear that loose coupling, clear contracts, and a disciplined approach to error handling are essential. I saw how good design kept systems resilient, not just in code but in the way users perceived and trusted the software. With every new version, from the days of .NET Framework through .NET Core and into .NET 9, I've found new ways to learn and improve my skills. The new language features, better tools, and a solid group of developers made me feel like I was building for more than just myself, but for a community of people who also care about quality.

If I had this book when I started, it would've been a huge help. I'd love to see a book that's got a practical, interactive walk from the basics to the advanced stuff, with real code and real applications at every step. Think of it as a record of problems encountered, lessons learned, and ideas made tangible. Even if you're just starting out with .NET or want to level up your skills for today's web development challenges, grab a seat, and let's dive in! Each chapter is designed to leave you with the answers and the confidence to tackle whatever challenges come your way.

Content

Preface .... *xvi*

GitforGits .... *xvii*

Acknowledgement .... *xviii*

Chapter 1: .NET 9, Tools and Sample App **1**

Overview *2*

Understanding .NET 9, SDKs, and Runtimes *2*

Familiarize with .NET 9 SDK 2

SDK vs Runtime 3

Target Frameworks 3

Exploring .NET CLI on Windows 4

Using Windows Terminal to Inspect Installs 5

Interpreting Output 6

Verifying Development Environment *6*

Creating Console Project 7

Building Console App 7

Running Console App 8

Introducing Deliberate Error and Observing Failure 8

Confirming SDK in Both Environments 9

Tuning IDE and Editor *10*

Configuring VS Code 10

Install C# Dev Kit Extension 10

Install NuGet Package Manager and Other Extensions 11

Key Preferences and Settings 11

Enable Format on Save 11

Configure Auto Save 11

Enable Breadcrumbs for Navigation 11

Tune Tab Size and Indentation 11

Code Completion and IntelliSense 12

Key Navigations 12

Go to Definition 12

Peek Definition 12

Go to Implementation 12

Go Back/Go Forward 12

Refactoring with VS Code 12

Rename Symbol 13

Extract Method 13

Change Signature and Add Parameter 13
Configuring Debug 13

Introducing End to End 'Trackr' App *14*
Why Build Trackr? 14
Sketching Trackr's Architecture 14
ASP.NET Core Web API Backend 14
SQL Server Express Database 15
WPF MVVM Desktop Client 15
Data and Workflow 15
Defining Task Entity 16

Summary *17*

Chapter 2: C# Fundamentals with a Console Task Tracker 18

Overview *19*

Main Method, Console I/O, and Menu Loop *19*
The Main Method 19
Writing to Console 20
Reading Input from Console 20
if and switch Statements 21
Building Menu Loop 22
Testing Menu Loop 24

Domain Model Basics *25*
Defining Simple TaskItem Class 25
Managing In-Memory List of Tasks 26
Adding Task 27
Listing All Tasks 27
Marking Task as Complete 28
Updating Menu 29

Working with Types, Nullability, and Simple Validation *30*
Enabling Nullable Reference Types 30
Updating TaskItem Class for Nullability 31
Applying Simple Validation during Task Creation 32
Handling Bad User Input 33

Collections and LINQ Queries *34*
Reviewing In-Memory Task List 34
Filtering Tasks using LINQ 34
Searching Tasks 35
Sorting Tasks 36
Connecting LINQ Features to Menu 37

Refactoring Console Logic into Methods and Classes *38*
Moving Menu Logic into ShowMenu Method 38

Extracting Input Handling to Separate Methods 39
Introducing TaskService Class 40
Final Refactored Program.cs 43

Summary ***45***

Chapter 3: Debugging and Troubleshooting .NET 9 Code 46

Overview ***47***

Attaching Debugger and Stepping Logic ***47***
Placing Breakpoints 47
Starting Debugging Session 48
Stepping Into and Over Methods 48
Experiencing Call Stack Window 49
Inspecting and Modifying Variables 49
Setting Conditional Breakpoints 50

Inspecting Variables and Evaluating Expressions ***50***
Locals, Autos, and Watch 51
Locals Window 51
Autos Window 51
Watch Window 51
Inspecting Variable Values while Paused 52
Evaluating Simple Expressions 52

Understanding Exceptions and Stack Traces ***52***
Intentionally Causing Exceptions 53
Null Reference Exception 53
Invalid Input Exception 53
Allowing Exceptions to Propagate and Observing Stack Traces 54
Reading Stack Trace and Jumping to Source Lines 55

Adding Basic Logging ***55***
Configuring Logging with Built-In Abstractions 56
Passing Logger to TaskService 56
Logging Key Actions 57

Fixing Bug ***59***
Inserting Subtle Bug 60
Reproducing Bug 60
Observing Bug Symptoms using Logging 61
Debugging for Root Cause 61
Fixing Bug and Verifying Solution 61

Summary ***62***

Chapter 4: Working with Existing .NET Applications 63

Overview 64

Navigating Unknown Codebase 64
Scanning Prebuilt .NET Solution 64
Open Solution 64
Recognize Main Components 64
Mapping Projects to Responsibilities 65
Exploring Folders and File Responsibilities 65
Definitions, References, and Call Sites 66
Go to Definition 66
Peek Definition 66
Find All References 66
Go to Implementation 66
Mapping Components to Responsibilities 66
Fast Exploration 67
Application Mental Model 67

Reproducing and Logging Existing Bugs 67
Identifying Bug 68
Reproducing Bug 68
Find Feature in Codebase 68
Trigger the Bug 68
Adding Targeted Logs and Assertions 68
Adding Targeted Logs 68
Adding Assertion 69
Observing Bug with Enabled Logs 70

Debugging across Layers (UI, API, and Data) 70
Attaching Debugger 70
Following Request 71
Place Breakpoints in each Layer 71
Initiate Operation from UI 71
Inspecting State at Boundary 71
At UI Layer 71
At Service Layer 72
At Data Layer 72
Diagnosing Layers Issues 72

Applying Safe Refactorings in Legacy Code 73
Spotting Opportunities for Refactoring 73
Extracting Methods 74
Introducing Helper Classes 75
Checking for Behavior Changes 76

Summary 76

Chapter 5: Revisiting ASP.NET Core and HTTP Basics 77

Overview 78

HTTP Requests and Responses *78*
What Is ASP.NET Core? 78
Understanding HTTP Request-Response Cycle 79
Controllers and Routing 79
Middleware Overvieew 80
Creating Task via HTTP 81

Building Minimal ASP.NET Core App *81*
Creating Web Service 82
Program Structure 82
Adding Simple Endpoint 82
Running Web Service 83
Inspecting Program.cs Pipeline 84
Sample Program 84

HTTP Request Pipeline and Middleware *85*
Adding Custom Middleware 85
Observing Real-Time Flow 86
Returning Response 86
Order and Interaction 87
Built-in Middleware 87

Registering Services with DI Container *88*
Refactoring TaskService 88
Registering TaskService in DI Container 90
Injecting TaskService into Controllers 90
Running and Testing Integration 91

Configuration and Environments *92*
Reading Configuration 92
Overriding Configuration per Environment 93
Add Environment-Specific Settings file 94
Run in Specific Environment 94
Checking Current Environment at Runtime 94

Summary *95*

Chapter 6: Routing and Web API Controllers 97

Overview *98*

Configuring Endpoint Routing *98*
Wiring up MapControllers 98
Testing Controller Discovery and Endpoint Mapping 99
Viewing Active Routes at Runtime 99
Add Endpoint Routing Diagnostics Middleware 99
Check Active Endpoints 100

Attribute Routing on Controllers and Actions *101*

Creating TasksController 101
Adding Route Attributes with Parameters 102
Testing URL Patterns and Routing 103

Designing Web API Controllers with [ApiController] 104
Annotating Controller with [ApiController] 104
Automatic Model Binding and Validation 105
Convenient and Safe Model Binding 106

Model Binding from Route, Query, and Body 107
Binding from Route Segments 107
Binding from Query Strings 108
Binding from Body (JSON) 108
Combining Binding Sources 109

Returning Results, Status Codes, and Problem Details 110
Returning Success 110
200 OK 110
201 Created 111
204 No Content 111
Returning Not Found (404) 111
Bad Request with Problem Details (400) 112

Summary 113

Chapter 7: Up and Running with SQL Server Express 115

Overview 116

Setting up SQL Server Express 116
Installing SQL Server Express 116
Setting up SQL Server Management Studio (SSMS) 117
Creating New Database and Simple Query 117

Designing Tables for Tasks and Related Entities 118
Creating Tasks Table 118
Designing Categories Table 119
Designing Users Table 119
Adding Foreign Keys 119
Inserting Task with Relationships 120

Writing Core SQL for Task Domain 120
Inserting New Tasks 121
Selecting Tasks 121
Joining Tasks to Related Tables 121
Updating Tasks 122
Deleting Tasks 123
Combining Filtering, Sorting, and Limits 123

Transactions and Integrity Constraints 123
Wrapping Multiple Operations Inside Transaction 123
Working with Integrity Constraints 124
Primary Key and Not Null Constraints 125
Foreign Key Constraints 125
Unique Constraints 125
Observing Database Enforcement 125

Connecting ADO.NET from Console Utility 126
Setting up Project 126
Crafting Connection String 126
Writing Core Utility 127
Running and Observing Utility 129
Updating and Deleting Tasks 129

Summary 130

Chapter 8: Working with Entity Framework Core 131

Overview 132

DbContext and Entity Classes 132
Add EF Core Packages 132
Create Simple Entity Classes 132
Create TaskDbContex 134
Connecting and Inserting Data 134

Configuring Mappings and Relationships 136
Data Annotations 136
More Control wtith Fluent API 138

Creating and Applying Migrations 139
Creating Initial Migration 139
Applying Migration to Generate DB Schema 140
Making Change 140
Creating and Applying Second Migration 140

Querying LINQ and Inspecting SQL 141
Querying with LINQ 141
Fetch Tasks 141
Filtering and Ordering Tasks 142
Joining with Related Entities 142
Inspecting Generated SQL 143
Logging SQL to Console 143
Inspecting SQL in Code 143

Handling Common Pitfalls 144
Inserting Entities 144
Updating Entities 145

Deleting Entities 146
Tracking Issues 146
Missing Includes 147

Summary 148

Chapter 9: Building Backend with ASP.NET Core and EF Core 149

Overview 150

Layering Controllers, Services, and Repositories 150
Creating Repository Layer 151
Developing Service Layer 153
Building Controller Layer 155
Registering Layers with DI 157

Implementing Repository Methods 157
Setting up Task Repository Interface 157
Fetching All Tasks 158
Finding Task by ID 158
Adding New Task 158
Updating an Existing Task 159
Deleting a Task 159

Wiring Services and Repositories through DI 160
Registering Repositories and Services in DI Container 160
Injecting Dependencies into Controllers 160

Defining API Contracts for Task Operations 162
Defining DTOs for Task Operations 162
TaskCreateDto 162
TaskUpdateDto 162
TaskListDto / TaskDetailDto 163
Mapping DTOs to Entities and Back 163
From DTO to Entity (Create and Update) 163
From Entity to DTO (List/Detail) 164
Using DTOs in the Controller 165

Validation, Error Handling, and Logging 166
Input Validation 166
Using Data Annotations on DTOs 166
Custom Validation Logic 167
Centralized Exception Handling 167
Structured Logging across API 168

Summary 169

Chapter 10: Decoupled Code with Interfaces and Dependency Injection 170

Overview......171

Spotting Tight Coupling in Backend and Client......171
Controllers Instantiating Concrete Classes......171
Direct Data Access in Services or Controllers......172
Client Code Bound to API Response Details......172
Services That Depend on Other Concrete Services......173

Defining Interfaces for Core Services and Repositories......174
Defining Repository Interfaces......174
Defining Service Interfaces......175
Refactoring Concrete Classes to Depend on Interfaces......175
Repository Implementation......175
Service Implementation......176
Updating Dependency Injection Registration......176
Refactoring Controllers and Consumers......177

Advanced DI Lifetimes and Scopes......177
Transient Lifetime......178
Scoped Lifetime......178
Singleton Lifetime......179

Testing with Fake and Mock Implementation......179
What Are Fakes and Mocks?......179
Creating Fake Repository......180
Testing with Fake Repository......181
Using Mocks for Behavior Verification......182
Simulating Failures and Edge Cases......182

Summary......182

Chapter 11: MVVM and WPF Desktop Client Basics......184

Overview......185

Positioning MVVM......185

Creating WPF Project......186
Creating WPF Project......187
Running Default Window......187
Connecting Project to Trackr......187
Building Familiarity with WPF Project Structure......188

Implementing ViewModels with INotifyPropertyChanged......188
Implementing TaskListViewModel......188
Wiring Property Change Notifications......189
Exposing Observable Collections for Binding......190
Connecting to View......190

Data Binding and Commands in XAML......191

Binding XAML Controls to ViewModel Properties......191
Adding Commands for Actions......192
Completing Tasks with Commands......194

Showing Tasks from an In Memory Service......*196*
Building In-Memory Task Service......196
Connecting ViewModel the Service......197

Summary......*199*

Chapter 12: Connecting WPF Client to Web API......200

Overview......*201*

Switching WPF Client from In-Memory to HTTP......*201*
Designing HttpClient Service for Web API Calls......201
Configuring HttpClient and Injecting Service......202
Making ViewModel Robust against Network Issues......203

Handling Serialization and Deserialization of DTOs......*204*
Serializing DTOs to JSON for Requests......204
Deserializing JSON Responses to ViewModel-Friendly Objects......205
Binding Deserialized Objects to ViewModel......206
Handling Serialization Settings......206
Validating JSON Payloads......206

Managing State and Refreshing the UI after API Calls......*207*
Updating ViewModel Collections......207
Managing Loading Indicators in UI......208

Graceful Error Handling in Desktop Client......*210*
Handling HTTP Failures......210
Handling Timeouts......211
Handling Validation Errors from Backend......211
Disabling Actions during Errors......213

Summary......*213*

Chapter 13: Deployment, Configuration, and Maintenance......215

Overview......*216*

Building and Publishing .NET 9 Applications......*216*
Publishing ASP.NET Core Web API......216
Publishing Web API Project......216
Creating Self-Contained Deployment......217
Publishing WPF Desktop Client......217

Hosting Web API......*217*
Running Web API behind Kestrel......218

Configuring IIS as Reverse Proxy 218
Install IIS and Required Modules..... 218
Configure IIS Site 219
Configure Reverse Proxy Handler..... 219

Managing Environments and App Settings..... 219
Configuring Development and Production Settings..... 220
Organizing Configuration files 220
Selecting Active Environment..... 221
Using Environment Variables 221
Switching Settings at Runtime..... 221
Sample Implementation 222

Monitoring with Logs and Health Checks 223
Designing and Exposing Health Checks..... 223
Register Health Checks in API..... 223
Map Health Endpoint..... 223
Integrating Rich, Structured Logging..... 224
Setting up Logging..... 224
Using ILogger..... 224

Summary 225

Index 226

Epilogue 228

Preface

For any .NET developer or C# programmer looking to build reliable, modern web applications using the latest advancements in the .NET platform, this book is an absolute must-have. Through practical scenarios, this book provides clear, step-by-step guidance, covering everything from the fundamentals of C# and .NET 9 to robust backend services and responsive desktop clients.

As you read, you will learn to set up development environment on Windows, build console applications, and advance to ASP.NET Core Web APIs. The book uses real-world examples to illuminate every concept, so you can learn debugging, troubleshooting, and the principles behind well-structured code. You will learn to work with SQL Server Express and integrate database operations seamlessly using Entity Framework Core. It also thoroughly covers the design of RESTful web APIs, dependency injection, and decoupled architectures, as well as the essentials of MVVM and WPF for creating user-friendly desktop clients. With each step, you will connect these clients to your Web API, manage data exchanges, handle errors, and implement essential features such as logging and health checks.

Each chapter is designed to develop practical skills, with each topic closely linked to professional software development practices. You won't find any shortcuts or hype here. It's just practical knowledge and tools to help you develop, deploy, and maintain modern .NET web applications with confidence.

In this book you will learn to:

- Explore the structure, build and the execution of .NET 9 applications using SDK, CLI, and runtime model.
- Translate problem statements into working C# logic using console apps and control flow.
- Acquire debugging skills using breakpoints, call stacks, logging, and exception analysis.
- Design clean ASP.NET Core Web APIs with routing, controllers, status codes, and validation.
- Workaround dependency injection and interfaces.
- Work directly with SQL Server and learn to enforce data integrity.
- Use Entity Framework Core for mappings, migrations, querying, and change tracking.
- Built backend with clear separation between controllers, services, and repositories.
- Implement WPF MVVM client with a Web API and staying synchronized with server state.
- Publish, configure, monitor, and operate .NET applications in real environments.

GitforGits

Prerequisites

No matter if you're just starting out with .NET or want to level up your skills for today's web development challenges, this book is the perfect guide to shape your needs and the career too.

Codes Usage

Are you in need of some helpful code examples to assist you in your programming and documentation? Look no further! Our book offers a wealth of supplemental material, including code examples and exercises.

Not only is this book here to aid you in getting your job done, but you have our permission to use the example code in your programs and documentation. However, please note that if you are reproducing a significant portion of the code, we do require you to contact us for permission.

But don't worry, using several chunks of code from this book in your program or answering a question by citing our book and quoting example code does not require permission. But if you do choose to give credit, an attribution typically includes the title, author, publisher, and ISBN. For example, ".NET 9 for Web Developers by Labio Cruz".

If you are unsure whether your intended use of the code examples falls under fair use or the permissions outlined above, please do not hesitate to reach out to us at support@gitforgits.com.

We are happy to assist and clarify any concerns.

Acknowledgement

I owe a tremendous debt of gratitude to GitforGits, for their unflagging enthusiasm and wise counsel throughout the entire process of writing this book. Their knowledge and careful editing helped make sure the piece was useful for people of all reading levels and comprehension skills. In addition, I'd like to thank everyone involved in the publishing process for their efforts in making this book a reality. Their efforts, from copyediting to advertising, made the project what it is today.

Finally, I'd like to express my gratitude to everyone who has shown me unconditional love and encouragement throughout my life. Their support was crucial to the completion of this book. I appreciate your help with this endeavour and your continued interest in my career.

Chapter 1: .NET 9, Tools and Sample App

Overview

The goal of this chapter is to set up our working environment for .NET 9 development on Windows and lay the foundation for everything that follows. In this chapter, we'll dive into what the .NET 9 SDK brings to our development toolkit and break down the differences between it and the runtime. It'll teach us to confirm which SDK and runtimes are on the machine and how the target framework of a project affects the code we write and run. We'll move hands-on by creating and building a minimal console project, running it, and introducing a small error so we can see how .NET surfaces problems and how to resolve them.

After that, you'll learn to set Visual Studio Code as our main editor, so it's all set for code completion, navigation, and debugging. You'll also learn to customize it for a smoother workflow. To wrap things up, you'll get to check out our Trackr sample app and see how it's put together. It's got a Web API backend, SQL Server Express database, and a WPF MVVM desktop client. Once you're done with this chapter, you'll be all set to start building and growing real .NET 9 applications. You'll have the right tools and mindset.

Understanding .NET 9, SDKs, and Runtimes

.NET 9 is a solid foundation for building all sorts of applications, from modern ones to console utilities, desktop GUIs, APIs, and even cloud and enterprise-level microservices. And Microsoft has positioned .NET as a "one platform, many workloads" ecosystem. The promise is simple, really. It's that we can code in C# (or F# or Visual Basic), share libraries across projects, and expect that our work will run efficiently on Windows, in the cloud, or on user desktops. To really use .NET 9 well, we need to understand several things, like what happens when we install the .NET 9 SDK, how it differs from the runtime, and how these elements come together to power our project files and build process.

For now, we're sticking with Windows as our go-to environment. All CLI instructions and outputs will use Windows Terminal as the shell, so there's no confusion about where to type commands or what prompts should look like.

Familiarize with .NET 9 SDK

The SDK is our developer toolbox. When we download and install the .NET 9 SDK on Windows, we are not just receiving a compiler, rather we are also receiving a carefully organized kit that allows us to do every part of development, from "new project" all the way to deployment.

Our SDK generally includes:

- The compilers for C#, F#, and Visual Basic, which translate our source code into IL (Intermediate Language) for the .NET runtime.
- The entire .NET CLI, surfaced as the **`dotnet`** command, which manages building,

running, testing, publishing, and even creating new projects from templates.

- All the core runtimes that match the SDK's version, .NET 9's runtime, the ASP.NET Core runtime for building web APIs and sites, and the Windows Desktop runtime, so we can build WPF or Windows Forms apps out of the box.
- Templates for quickly starting common project types: console, web API, class library, test, and desktop applications.
- The default set of .NET libraries (sometimes called the Base Class Library or BCL), which brings in features like file handling, networking, collections, cryptography, threading, XML/JSON parsing, and much more.

Now, once the SDK is installed, our Windows machine is fully prepared to build and run any application that targets .NET 9. We can spin up a new project, build it, test it, and publish it for use on another Windows system that has at least the correct runtime.

SDK vs Runtime

This distinction trips up even some experienced developers. The ***SDK*** is for development, while the ***runtime*** is for running compiled applications. I will tell we what this means on our system:

- If we have only the runtime installed, we can execute .NET apps that were built elsewhere, but we cannot compile new code or generate new projects.
- If we have the SDK installed, we get everything in the runtime plus the full suite of developer tools.

The runtime itself includes only those components that allow a .NET application to execute, memory management, garbage collection, JIT (just-in-time) compilation, and support libraries required at execution time. The SDK, on the other hand, is the superset, which brings the runtime plus compilers, CLI, and templates.

You may think of SDK as the full kitchen and the runtime as just the oven. We need the kitchen to bake something new; whereas someone else may only desire to have the oven to heat up what we prepared.

SO, if we attempt to use a development command such as **`dotnet new`** or **`dotnet build`** on a system that has only the runtime, we will see errors saying the SDK is missing. On a machine with the SDK installed, both development and execution are possible.

Target Frameworks

Every .NET project on Windows uses a project file with the **`.csproj`** extension to tell the SDK what it wants to target. And, within this file, there is a property called **`TargetFramework`** that defines which version of the .NET runtime our application is built against. In our book, we will consistently use:

```
<PropertyGroup>
  <TargetFramework>net9.0</TargetFramework>
</PropertyGroup>
```

This declaration tells the SDK that when we build our project, it should reference .NET 9's libraries and APIs, and the output should be expected to run on the .NET 9 runtime. If we accidentally set this to a version that is not installed on our machine, builds will fail, or the application will not launch until the correct runtime is present.

The developers who build libraries for use in more than one runtime can specify multiple frameworks:

```
<PropertyGroup>
  <TargetFrameworks>net9.0;net8.0</TargetFrameworks>
</PropertyGroup>
```

This will tell the SDK to build the project for both .NET 9 and .NET 8. Each output is compiled for its respective runtime, which is helpful for producing NuGet packages or libraries with broad compatibility.

Exploring .NET CLI on Windows

We focus now on the ***.NET CLI***, which is central to our workflow. After installing the SDK, we then try to gain access to the **`dotnet`** command everywhere on Windows through Windows Terminal.

The .NET CLI is responsible for:

- Creating new projects (**`dotnet new`**)
- Restoring dependencies (**`dotnet restore`**)
- Building projects (**`dotnet build`**)
- Running apps (**`dotnet run`**)
- Publishing for deployment (**`dotnet publish`**)
- Running unit tests (**`dotnet test`**)

So here, whenever we type a dotnet command, the CLI looks for the appropriate SDK to service the request. If our project targets net9.0, it seeks out the .NET 9 SDK and runtime. The CLI will always prefer the highest installed version that matches the target, unless a specific configuration or global.json file directs it otherwise.

Using Windows Terminal to Inspect Installs

Now next is, that we learn to confirm our environment. Now before we proceed, and as said previously, we need to make a note that we will be using Windows Terminal as our default CLI throughout the entire book, since it provides an excellent tabbed interface, unicode support, and integrates smoothly with modern Windows.

So, let us begin. To inspect our .NET installation, we will open the terminal and type:

```
dotnet --info
```

This command outputs detailed information about the .NET environment. Given below is a sample of what we might see:

```
.NET SDK (reflecting any global.json):
 Version:   9.0.100
 Commit:    62be57b3ab
Runtime Environment:
 OS Name:     Windows
 OS Version:  10.0.22621
 OS Platform: Windows
 RID:         win10-x64
 Base Path:   C:\Program Files\dotnet\sdk\9.0.100\
Host:
  Version:      9.0.0
  Architecture: x64
  Commit:       f5718f35ae
.NET SDKs installed:
  9.0.100 [C:\Program Files\dotnet\sdk]
  8.0.200 [C:\Program Files\dotnet\sdk]
.NET runtimes installed:
  Microsoft.NETCore.App 9.0.0 [C:\Program
Files\dotnet\shared\Microsoft.NETCore.App]
  Microsoft.AspNetCore.App 9.0.0 [C:\Program
Files\dotnet\shared\Microsoft.AspNetCore.App]
```

```
  Microsoft.WindowsDesktop.App 9.0.0 [C:\Program
Files\dotnet\shared\Microsoft.WindowsDesktop.App]
```

This output confirms:

- The active SDK version is **`9.0.100`**;
- All SDKs available on the machine;
- The OS and platform (always useful to confirm if running on Windows and the architecture is correct); and
- Every installed runtime and the directories they are loaded from

If we do not see the target SDK or runtime in the list, then the installation is incomplete or the system path is misconfigured.

Interpreting Output

This diagnostic output is more like a map to our .NET environment. If we are about to clone a project from source control and it targets net9.0, then seeing the **`Microsoft.NETCore.App 9.0.0`** and **`9.0.100`** in the SDKs installed means our machine is fully ready. If our project targets net8.0, but we only see net9.0 listed, we know a quick SDK or runtime install may be needed.

So whenever troubleshooting, we must always try to start by running **`dotnet --info`** in the terminal. If a build or run fails due to missing components, this output shows exactly what is available. If a deployment fails on a server, comparing **`dotnet --info`** from the development machine and the server will help identify version mismatches immediately.

When we build a project, the SDK compiles our source against the target framework declared in the **`.csproj`** file. The build process checks the machine for an appropriate SDK and runtime. If the SDK is present, building and running the application locally is seamless. When we publish and deploy, the application expects the same or compatible runtime to be available on the target system. The overall project file serves as a contract, since it tells the SDK what the project expects, and it is up to us to make sure the environment matches.

Verifying Development Environment

Now, before we dive into any real-world development, I rather recommend to confirm that our setup works from end to end. And, we can do this by creating the simplest possible .NET project, a blank console app, building it, running it, and observing both success and deliberate failure. If we do this, it will show us that the environment is ready, and on top of it, it also shows what healthy and unhealthy feedback looks like from .NET and our IDE.

Creating Console Project

We begin by opening the windows terminal. To start with, we create a new folder by typing:

```
mkdir DotnetLearning
cd DotnetLearning
```

Next, we then create a new console project targeting .NET 9 by running:

```
dotnet new console -n MinimalConsole
```

Here,

- **`dotnet new console`** creates a new C# console application from the default template.
- **`-n MinimalConsole`** specifies the project name and creates a folder named **`MinimalConsole`** in the current directory.

Next, we then move into the project directory:

```
cd MinimalConsole
```

If we look inside this folder, we will find a file named **`Program.cs`** and a project file called **`MinimalConsole.csproj`**. This is the default skeleton for every .NET console app.

Building Console App

Now here, we want to make sure the code compiles and the SDK is functioning as expected. For this, we will build the project by running the following command:

```
dotnet build
```

If everything is healthy, the output in the terminal will look like the following:

```
 Determining projects to restore...
  Restored
C:\Users\YourName\DotnetLearning\MinimalConsole\MinimalConsole
.csproj (in 120 ms).
  MinimalConsole ->
C:\Users\YourName\DotnetLearning\MinimalConsole\bin\Debug\net9
.0\MinimalConsole.dll
Build succeeded.
```

```
    0 Warning(s)
    0 Error(s)
Time Elapsed 00:00:01.23
```

In the above output, the key messages here are "Build succeeded." and "0 Error(s)". as it tells us that the .NET 9 SDK is active and working correctly.

Running Console App

To execute the newly built console application, type:

```
dotnet run
```

This command compiles the application, launches it immediately and the template project prints "Hello, World!" to the terminal as following:

```
Hello, World!
```

If there were errors in the build or run steps, .NET would display clear error messages, usually with file names and line numbers.

Introducing Deliberate Error and Observing Failure

To troubleshoot, it's useful to see how .NET responds to problems. I'll introduce a small mistake in the code, rebuild, and watch how the tooling directs us to fix it.

- For this, we will open the **`Program.cs`** and will use ***Visual Studio 2022*** as our default IDE throughout this book.
- Within the Visual Studio, we will then double-click the **`Program.cs`** in the Solution Explorer.

Here, we will change the existing line from:

```
Console.WriteLine("Hello, World!");
```

to:

```
Console.WriteLinez("Hello, World!");
```

The typo, adding a 'z' to the method name, introduces a syntax error. Now, return to the terminal and rebuild:

```
dotnet build
```

The output will resemble:

```
Program.cs(3,1): error CS0117: 'Console' does not contain a
definition for 'WriteLinez'
[C:\Users\YourName\DotnetLearning\MinimalConsole\MinimalConsol
e.csproj]

Build FAILED.

Program.cs(3,1): error CS0117: 'Console' does not contain a
definition for 'WriteLinez'
[C:\Users\YourName\DotnetLearning\MinimalConsole\MinimalConsol
e.csproj]

    0 Warning(s)

    1 Error(s)

Time Elapsed 00:00:00.45
```

This shows that .NET's compiler is precise. It gives the file name, line number, and even the error code (**`CS0117`** in this case). We see immediately where the problem lies.

To fix the typo, we will then save the file and rebuild:

```
dotnet build
```

This time, "Build succeeded." returns, which thereby confirms the fix.

Now here, if we want to make sure that our IDE is also wired correctly, we need to run the program inside ***Visual Studio 2022***. And for this, we will open the **`MinimalConsole`** solution. And, in the toolbar, we will set the build configuration to "Debug" and the target is set to "net9.0". After this, we then click the "Start" button (the green play arrow) or press **`F5`**.

The Output window or the inbuilt console should display:

```
Hello, World!
```

If we see this message, Visual Studio is building and running the project using the same SDK and runtime as the CLI. If a build error remains from our earlier typo, Visual Studio's Error List will display a message nearly identical to what we saw in the terminal.

Confirming SDK in Both Environments

We want to be certain that both the CLI and the IDE are using the .NET 9 SDK, and not an older version. So here, the surest way to check is to look at the build output and project properties.

- In the terminal, after **`dotnet build`**, the output path will include **`net9.0`**.

- And, in Visual Studio, right-click the project in Solution Explorer, select "Properties," and verify the Target Framework is set to ".NET 9.0".

Additionally, we can run the following command:

```
dotnet --list-sdks
```

And in Visual Studio, we need to select ***Help > About Microsoft Visual Studio***. Here, we shall confirm that the .NET SDK version listed includes 9.0.x.

This cycle of create, build, run, observe errors, fix, rerun, is the essential workflow for every .NET developer. It proves our windows development environment is healthy and wired for success. After this, we can confidently move on, knowing any issues that arise later are not because of a broken foundation, but from the challenges of real application logic ahead.

Tuning IDE and Editor

As for development, we've decided that VS Code is going to be our go-to tool for the whole project. This is a smart choice, no doubt. The VS Code is lightweight, fast, and highly customizable. With the right extensions, it provides a development experience that's almost as powerful as a full IDE. So, our plan is to set up VS Code so that we spend most of our time thinking about code and not about the editor. With the right setup, code completion, navigation, and debugging become smooth, so problems in our apps are what challenge us, not the environment.

Configuring VS Code

The first requirement here, is the correct extension set. By default, the VS Code does not come with C# or .NET support, but the Microsoft provides a first-class extension for this.

Install C# Dev Kit Extension

- Open VS Code.
- Go to the Extensions view by clicking the square icon on the left sidebar or pressing **`Ctrl+Shift+X`**.
- Search for ***"C# Dev Kit"*** and select the official extension by Microsoft.
- Click ***Install***.

This extension brings syntax highlighting and IntelliSense code completion, debugging for .NET projects, and solution support for .NET Core and .NET 9. It also has code navigation features like "Go to Definition" and "Peek Definition"

The C# Dev Kit will prompt to install any additional dependencies (such as .NET Runtime support) automatically, so allow any recommended installs.

Install NuGet Package Manager and Other Extensions

- Here, go to the Extensions view, and search for ***"NuGet Package Manager"*** and install it. This extension makes it much easier to manage dependencies for our projects directly inside VS Code.
- After this, search for and install the ***EditorConfig for VS Code*** extension. This helps enforce consistent formatting if the project uses **`.editorconfig`** files.
- In addition, we may also wish to install ***Prettier - Code Formatter*** for general formatting support across multiple languages.

Key Preferences and Settings

We want VS Code to work for us, not against us. There are some key settings that will optimize our experience with .NET 9 as shown below:

Enable Format on Save

- Press **`Ctrl+,`** to open Settings.
- In the search bar, type "format on save".
- Check the box for ***Editor: Format on Save***.

This thing ensures that our code is always tidy every time we save, making code reviews and teamwork much smoother.

Configure Auto Save

- In the Settings panel, search for "auto save".
- Choose the option "onWindowChange" or "afterDelay", depending on the preference.

This reduces accidental loss of work and keeps the codebase more up to date in collaborative scenarios.

Enable Breadcrumbs for Navigation

- Type "breadcrumbs" in the Settings search.
- Make sure ***Breadcrumbs: Enabled*** is checked.

The breadcrumbs show the current file, class, and method at the top of the editor window. It makes the navigation between large files and classes easier.

Tune Tab Size and Indentation

- Still in Settings, search for "tab size".
- Set ***Editor: Tab Size*** to **4** (which is the .NET default).
- Set ***Editor: Insert Spaces*** to true, ensuring that the Tab key inserts spaces instead of tab characters.

These defaults keep code style consistent with most .NET projects.

Code Completion and IntelliSense

Now that we have the C# Dev Kit installed, we can start typing in any **`.cs`** file, and very easily we can try the **`Console.`** Like here, we we will immediately see suggestions such as **`WriteLine`**, **`ReadLine`**, and other static members. The IntelliSense is context-aware, so as we define new variables, classes, and methods, the suggestions will grow more precise.

This IntelliSense is not just for method names, as it helps with parameter info, method overloads, and even documentation summaries. It reduces the time spent flipping between files or searching online for signatures.

Key Navigations

In the following, we will try out some of the core navigation features that accelerate daily development:

Go to Definition

- Place the cursor on any method or class name.
- Right-click and select ***Go to Definition***, or use the shortcut **`F12`**.

The VS Code jumps straight to where that symbol is defined, even if it is in another file or a referenced NuGet package.

Peek Definition

For this, just place the cursor on a symbol, right-click, and select ***Peek Definition*** (or use **`Alt+F12`**).

Here, we will see a small inline window appears with the definition. It allows us to reference the code without leaving our current context.

Go to Implementation

For this, we place the cursor on an interface or abstract method, right-click, and select ***Go to Implementation*** (**`Ctrl+F12`**).

The VS Code lists all concrete implementations of that interface or method within the project.

Go Back/Go Forward

After jumping to a definition, we then have to use **`Alt+LeftArrow`** to go back and **`Alt+RightArrow`** to go forward. This works like navigation history in a web browser.

Such feature eliminates endless scrolling and manual searches, especially as our codebase grows.

Refactoring with VS Code

VS Code, powered by the C# Dev Kit, provides several automated refactorings:

Rename Symbol

- Click on any variable, class, or method name.
- Press **`F2`**.
- Type a new name and press Enter.

All references to that symbol across the project will update instantly.

Extract Method

- Select a block of code.
- Right-click and select ***Refactor...*** or use the lightbulb that appears.
- Choose ***Extract Method***.

Here, the VS Code creates a new method with the selected code and replaces the original code with a call to the new method.

Change Signature and Add Parameter

- Here, we place the cursor on a method, then use the lightbulb menu or **`Ctrl+.`** to see quick fixes.
- And then, we choose options like ***Add parameter to method signature*** or ***Reorder parameters***.

All these refactoring features help keep our code clean, maintainable, and easy to extend.

Configuring Debug

The debugging in VS Code is quite straightforward, once we have the C# Dev Kit installed.

- Open the **`.csproj`** project in VS Code.
- Press **`F5`** to launch the debugger.
- VS Code will ask to select the environment. Choose ***.NET 9 (C#)***.
- The debugger attaches to the app, and we can:
  - Set breakpoints by clicking to the left of any line number.
  - Step through code using the toolbar at the top.
  - Inspect variables in the ***Variables*** pane.
  - Watch expressions, view call stacks, and see output in the Debug Console.

If the app prints **`Hello, World!`**, we should see this in the Debug Console. We can set a breakpoint on **`Console.WriteLine`** and step through to see execution in real time.

Now that VS Code is very well tuned for .NET 9, we can consider ourselves that we are well capable to focus entirely on our applications, and exploring problems and solutions, rather than just wrestling with our tools.

Introducing End to End 'Trackr' App

Now that we're diving into building real applications with .NET 9, it's key to ground all our learning in a concrete, relatable example. For our project, we're going to design and slowly put together a handy app called ***Trackr***. It's a simple but realistic task tracker. The Trackr program will walk us through all the main features of .NET 9, like creating a RESTful backend, working with a real database, and building a modern desktop client. Each chapter will add new depth to this system, and by the end, we'll see how all the pieces work together in a professional-grade workflow.

Why Build Trackr?

Almost every developer and team manage tasks. Sometimes this happens in spreadsheets, sticky notes, or email threads. By building a focused Task Tracker, we will address real-world requirements such as adding new tasks, tracking status, editing, deleting, and viewing a list of work items. This simple domain allows us to spend our energy learning architecture, APIs, data access, and UI, instead of getting lost in business rules.

The Trackr app is not just a toy. We will structure it to mimic what teams use in daily operations, so we will see the kinds of problems and solutions that apply to much larger systems. This approach ensures that as we add features, we gain habits and skills that translate to production work in companies and open-source projects alike.

Sketching Trackr's Architecture

Let us outline the three core components that make up Trackr:

ASP.NET Core Web API Backend

At the heart of Trackr is an ASP.NET Core Web API, built on .NET 9. This backend provides endpoints to create, read, update, and delete tasks (CRUD operations). The Web API acts as the central hub that clients, whether they are desktop applications, mobile apps, or other services, can interact with securely and reliably.

The main roles of this backend include:

- Exposing RESTful endpoints for managing tasks.
- Handling validation and business rules.
- Orchestrating data access to the underlying database.
- Supporting future extensions such as user authentication, reporting, or integrations.

All our business logic and data validation will live here, not in the client. This clear separation allows any front end to evolve without duplicating logic.

SQL Server Express Database

The data storage is handled by ***SQL Server Express***, which is the lightweight, free version of Microsoft's SQL Server engine. Every task, with its fields (such as title, status, due date, and description), will be persisted here.

This choice is intentional:

- SQL Server Express is easy to install and manage on Windows, and provides features we need for relational data, such as foreign keys, indexing, and transactions.
- We can grow our schema as requirements evolve, introducing new fields or tables as needed.
- Using a real database, instead of in-memory lists or files, means we are building habits and workflows that match what professional development teams use daily.

The Entity Framework Core, Microsoft's modern Object Relational Mapper (ORM), will act as our bridge between C# code and the SQL Server database. This lets us write strongly-typed queries in C#, while the framework generates SQL and handles connections behind the scenes.

WPF MVVM Desktop Client

While web frontends are common, the desktop applications are still critical for many workflows, especially in organizations where speed, advanced UI, or offline support is required. So, for this, we will use the ***WPF (Windows Presentation Foundation)*** for our Trackr client building on the ***MVVM (Model-View-ViewModel)*** pattern.

Our WPF desktop client will:

- Display lists of tasks, with sorting and filtering options.
- Allow users to add, edit, and delete tasks.
- Communicate with the backend Web API over HTTP using JSON.
- Showcase modern data binding, command patterns, and separation of concerns through MVVM.

The WPF let us demonstrate how a desktop application can feel modern, reactive, and fully in sync with a cloud-powered backend.

Data and Workflow

Let us visualize how the pieces of Trackr talk to each other. For example, if a user opens the Trackr desktop client and wants to add a new task:

1. ***User action***: The user fills out a form and clicks "Add Task."
2. ***WPF MVVM Client***: The ViewModel packages the data as a JSON object and sends it

as an HTTP POST to the Web API.

3. ***ASP.NET Core Web API***: The backend receives the request, validates the input, applies business rules, and (using Entity Framework Core) writes the new task to SQL Server Express.
4. ***SQL Server Express***: The database stores the new row and returns confirmation to the backend.
5. ***Response***: The Web API responds with the details of the created task, which the WPF client shows in the task list.

This pattern repeats for every action, editing, deleting, or listing tasks. The Web API remains the single source of truth, so all clients share the same data and business logic.

Defining Task Entity

Before we write code, we can think of what a task in Trackr looks like. Each task will have:

- ***Id*** (integer, unique)
- ***Title*** (short description)
- ***Description*** (optional, longer notes)
- ***Status*** (for example: "Pending", "In Progress", "Completed")
- ***DueDate*** (optional, datetime)
- ***CreatedAt*** (datetime, set automatically)
- ***UpdatedAt*** (datetime, set when the task is changed)

Here, we may add fields later, but these cover most real-world needs. Our database schema, C# models, and API endpoints will all reflect this structure.

In the following chapters, each chapter will extend the Trackr app one step further:

- First, we will design the database schema and data models.
- Next, we will scaffold the Web API, implement endpoints, and secure the data flow.
- We will wire up Entity Framework Core to persist and query tasks.
- Later, we will create the WPF desktop client, build the MVVM layers, and bind the UI to our data.
- We will practice debugging, refactoring, and extending both backend and client to support new features.
- At every point, the system will work as a real application, not just isolated code samples.

The way Trackr is set up is similar to how production .NET applications are set up in general. We separated the backend, database, and client, and we're seeing great results. As we move forward, remember this roadmap. Each chapter and feature will feel like another piece of Trackr falling into place. By the end, we will have built a cohesive, maintainable, and modern .NET 9 solution on Windows, one that gives us confidence for future projects and real-world work.

Summary

While reading this chapter, I'm sure you'll agree that we've got a solid understanding of .NET 9 and its development environment on Windows. We figured out how the target framework in a project file determines the version of .NET our application expects, and how to confirm installed SDKs and runtimes with the **`dotnet --info`** command in the terminal. We did a practice run where we created a basic console project, built and ran it, and then checked the .NET reports for both success and errors. We saw how errors appear in both the CLI and Visual Studio Code through a deliberate coding mistake, and we learned how to resolve them. Next, we customized VS Code with essential extensions, preferences, and navigation shortcuts to boost productivity, focusing on features like code completion, navigation, and debugging.

Finally, we introduced Trackr, our end-to-end sample Task Tracker application, and outlined its architecture using an ASP.NET Core Web API backend, SQL Server Express database, and a WPF MVVM desktop client. This chapter's steps made us feel good about our development environment, knowing it's reliable and ready for real projects.

CHAPTER 2: C# FUNDAMENTALS WITH A CONSOLE TASK TRACKER

Overview

In this chapter, we're going to take a hands-on, step-by-step approach to building a console-based task tracker using C# and .NET 9. To start, we'll build a basic interactive menu that asks for user input repeatedly, uses if and switch statements to make decisions, and keeps the application running until an exit command is given. We'll take a look at how to describe the core business concept by designing a TaskItem class and managing a growing list of tasks in memory. We'll practice safe programming by enabling nullable reference types and implementing simple but effective validation to catch empty input and prevent null-related issues. It'll walk us through working with collections and show us how to use LINQ queries to filter, search, and sort tasks. This makes it a breeze to find the info we need and change the data however we want.

Moving forward, we'll break down the logic into methods and then into a dedicated TaskService class. By doing this, we'll learn how to organize code for better clarity, testability, and future expansion. The end of the chapter will have you not only knowing the ropes of C# syntax, but also picking up some solid professional development habits that'll be a great stepping stone for more advanced .NET projects down the road.

Main Method, Console I/O, and Menu Loop

With so far, we have understood in the previous chapter, we will now begin turning the Trackr into a real, interactive console application. This topic teaches us how a .NET console program starts, how to read from and write to the console, and how to create a persistent menu that loops, listens for user input, and only exits when told to do so.

The Main Method

Just to let you know, every .NET console application begins execution at the **`Main`** method. In C#, the **`Main`** method acts as the application's entry point, where all code starts running. The template project we generated for Trackr created a **`Program.cs`** file, and inside it we find something like:

```
using System;
class Program
{
    static void Main(string[] args)
    {
        // Our code will go here.
    }
```

```
}
```

The **`Main`** method can receive arguments from the command line in the form of a string array called **`args`**. For most menu-driven apps, we do not need to use command line arguments, but it is good to know they are available if we ever need to extend the app to accept startup options.

So here, inside **`Main`**, we will write the code that will manage our application's lifecycle. We can also display instructions, read user input, process choices, and handle the logic for exiting the program.

Writing to Console

A menu-driven app lives and breathes by communicating clearly with its user. To display information, C# uses the **`Console.WriteLine`** method:

```
Console.WriteLine("Welcome to Trackr - Your Task Tracker!");
```

We will use this method often to print menus, prompts, and status messages. It adds a newline at the end of each message, keeping the console readable and user-friendly.

Next, when designing menus, clarity is key. For this, we will design a basic menu for our task tracker:

```
Console.WriteLine();
Console.WriteLine("==== Trackr Main Menu ====");
Console.WriteLine("1. List tasks");
Console.WriteLine("2. Add task");
Console.WriteLine("3. Delete task");
Console.WriteLine("4. Exit");
Console.Write("Enter the choice: ");
```

In the above, the use of blank lines and clear labels assist the user understand what options are available at every step.

Reading Input from Console

Once we present choices, we need to capture user input. The C# offers **`Console.ReadLine()`** to read a full line of text from the user. This returns a string, which we then need to parse or interpret as shown below:

```
string? input = Console.ReadLine();
```

Now here, the **Console.ReadLine()** can return **null** (if the input stream is closed), we often use the nullable type **string?**. And for the menu input, we usually expect a number, so we can try parsing it as an integer:

```
if (int.TryParse(input, out int choice))
{
    // Now we have a valid integer in 'choice'.
}
else
{
    Console.WriteLine("Invalid input. Please enter a
number.");
}
```

This method prevents the application from crashing when a user enters something unexpected, and it provides feedback that takes users back on track.

if and switch Statements

The menu-based applications rely on branching to decide what to do next. The **if** statement allows us to handle conditions that are not easily mapped to menu options, while the **switch** statement is a clean way to direct program flow based on the user's menu choice.

Following is a basic structure using **switch**:

```
switch (choice)
{
    case 1:
        ListTasks();
        break;
    case 2:
        AddTask();
        break;
    case 3:
        DeleteTask();
```

```
        break;
    case 4:
        Console.WriteLine("Exiting Trackr. Goodbye!");
        return; // Leaves the Main method and ends the app.
    default:
        Console.WriteLine("Please select a valid option.");
        break;
}
```

With this design, every menu option can easily map to a specific method. Also, this makes the code easy to read and maintain as we add more features.

Building Menu Loop

A single run of the menu is not enough. We need our program to repeatedly show the menu after each action, so users can keep working until they decide to exit. And for this, the best pattern is a **while** loop that continues until the user chooses the "Exit" option.

In the above, we will put all the pieces together:

```
using System;
class Program
{
    static void Main(string[] args)
    {
        bool running = true;
        while (running)
        {
            Console.WriteLine();
            Console.WriteLine("==== Trackr Main Menu ====");
            Console.WriteLine("1. List tasks");
            Console.WriteLine("2. Add task");
            Console.WriteLine("3. Delete task");
            Console.WriteLine("4. Exit");
```

```
        Console.Write("Enter the choice: ");
        string? input = Console.ReadLine();
        if (int.TryParse(input, out int choice))
        {
            switch (choice)
            {
                case 1:
                    ListTasks();
                    break;
                case 2:
                    AddTask();
                    break;
                case 3:
                    DeleteTask();
                    break;
                case 4:
                    Console.WriteLine("Exiting Trackr.
Goodbye!");
                    running = false;
                    break;
                default:
                    Console.WriteLine("Please select a
valid option.");
                    break;
            }
        }
        else
        {
            Console.WriteLine("Invalid input. Please enter
a number.");
```

```
            }
        }
    }
    static void ListTasks()
    {
        Console.WriteLine("[ListTasks not yet implemented]");
    }
    static void AddTask()
    {
        Console.WriteLine("[AddTask not yet implemented]");
    }
    static void DeleteTask()
    {
        Console.WriteLine("[DeleteTask not yet implemented]");
    }
}
```

From the above structure, our program will keep presenting the menu, handling input, and responding to actions until the user enters 4 to exit.

Testing Menu Loop

Finally, to check that our program works as expected, we will save the updated **`Program.cs`** file and run:

```
dotnet run
```

The output should look like this:

```
==== Trackr Main Menu ====
1. List tasks
2. Add task
3. Delete task
4. Exit
```

```
Enter the choice:
```

After this, we can enter numbers from 1 to 4. The menu repeats after each action, and only exits when 4 is entered.

If an invalid value is entered, such as "hello", the output will be:

```
Invalid input. Please enter a number.
```

If the user enters a valid number outside the range, the output will be:

```
Please select a valid option.
```

This simple loop provides a flexible pattern. Each menu option points to its own method, which can be filled in with more logic as we move forward. For now, the placeholder methods simply print a message, but soon, these will manage real data and connect to our growing Task Tracker features.

The use of **`while`** loop and a **`switch`** statement establish a strong pattern that will make adding, editing, and managing tasks straightforward. With new features are introduced, we only need to add menu options and connect them to new methods.

Domain Model Basics

The good stuff is, we're able to take abstract menu actions and turn them into real, trackable data. All systems that manage tasks, whether they're a massive enterprise platform or a weekend side project, start by describing the core "thing" they manage. In Trackr, that's a task. If we design a class that accurately reflects the business concept of a task, we'll end up with clear, maintainable code. We'll define a **`TaskItem`** class with fields for Id, Title, Status, and an optional DueDate. Then, we'll take care of a list of these tasks in memory and write methods to create, list, and mark tasks as completed.

Defining Simple TaskItem Class

To start with, we will keep our **`TaskItem`** class clear and basic. In the following, we will write it in a new file named **`TaskItem.cs`** in the same project folder:

```
public class TaskItem
{
    public int Id { get; set; }
    public string Title { get; set; }
```

```
    public bool IsCompleted { get; set; }
    public string? DueDate { get; set; } // Use string for due
date to keep things very simple
    public TaskItem(int id, string title, string? dueDate)
    {
        Id = id;
        Title = title;
        DueDate = dueDate;
        IsCompleted = false;
    }
}
```

In the above, each task has a number (**Id**), a description (**Title**), and a yes/no status (**IsCompleted**). And, the due date is optional, so we can use a nullable string for now.

Managing In-Memory List of Tasks

We can easily manage tasks using a list inside our main program. For this, we will add the following at the top of **Program.cs**, and before the **Main** method:

```
using System.Collections.Generic;
class Program
{
    static List<TaskItem> tasks = new List<TaskItem>();
    static int nextId = 1;
    static void Main(string[] args)
    {
        // Menu loop will go here
    }
    // Add other methods below
}
```

In the above, the **tasks** store every task we add, and the **nextId** keeps track of which number to assign to the next new task.

Adding Task

In the above example, we will add a new task using the simplest method:

```
static void AddTask()
{
    Console.Write("Enter task title: ");
    string title = Console.ReadLine();
    Console.Write("Enter due date (optional): ");
    string dueDate = Console.ReadLine();
    TaskItem newTask = new TaskItem(nextId, title,
string.IsNullOrWhiteSpace(dueDate) ? null : dueDate);
    tasks.Add(newTask);
    Console.WriteLine($"Task added with Id {nextId}.");
    nextId++;
}
```

In the above, we are asking for a title and an optional due date. And, the new task is added to the list, and the next available Id is used.

Listing All Tasks

A simple way to show every task in our list is as shown below:

```
static void ListTasks()
{
    if (tasks.Count == 0)
    {
        Console.WriteLine("No tasks found.");
        return;
    }
    foreach (var task in tasks)
    {
```

```
        string status = task.IsCompleted ? "Completed" :
"Pending";
        string due = task.DueDate ?? "No due date";
        Console.WriteLine($"Id: {task.Id}, Title:
{task.Title}, Status: {status}, Due: {due}");
    }
}
```

This above program prints each task's details, including status and due date.

Marking Task as Complete

Following is a simple method for marking a task complete:

```
static void CompleteTask()
{
    Console.Write("Enter Id of task to mark as complete: ");
    string input = Console.ReadLine();
    if (int.TryParse(input, out int id))
    {
        foreach (var task in tasks)
        {
            if (task.Id == id)
            {
                task.IsCompleted = true;
                Console.WriteLine("Task marked as
completed.");
                return;
            }
        }
        Console.WriteLine("Task not found.");
    }
    else
```

```
    {
        Console.WriteLine("Invalid input.");
    }
}
```

In the above, the user enters an Id. We find that task and update its status.

Updating Menu

The menu loop in **`Main`** now uses the following methods:

```
bool running = true;
while (running)
{
    Console.WriteLine("\n==== Trackr Menu ====");
    Console.WriteLine("1. List tasks");
    Console.WriteLine("2. Add task");
    Console.WriteLine("3. Complete task");
    Console.WriteLine("4. Exit");
    Console.Write("Choose an option: ");
    string input = Console.ReadLine();
    switch (input)
    {
        case "1":
            ListTasks();
            break;
        case "2":
            AddTask();
            break;
        case "3":
            CompleteTask();
            break;
```

```
        case "4":
            running = false;
            break;
        default:
            Console.WriteLine("Please choose a valid
option.");
            break;
    }
}
```

Now, you can run the app with **`dotnet run`**. After this, you can select option 2 to add a task, and then 1 to see the task in the list.

We can also select option 3, enter the task Id, then select 1 again and see the status now shows "Completed".

You can keep adding, viewing, and completing tasks as much as we wish.

By keeping each part simple and direct, we have now built a habit: describe the business concept clearly (as a class), and manage it with an in-memory list and straightforward methods. This pattern can be carried forward and improved step by step as we advance.

Working with Types, Nullability, and Simple Validation

As we keep building Trackr, it is important to prevent common bugs and confusion caused by missing or invalid data. The C# gives us tools to defend against these issues, such as ***nullable reference types*** and type-safe validation. These features and writing basic checks, protects our application from crashes and unpredictable behavior.

Enabling Nullable Reference Types

The C# allows us to control whether reference types like strings can be null. By default, the older code treats all reference types as nullable, which can cause runtime errors if we forget to check for nulls. However, with nullable reference types enabled, the C# can help us see where nulls might appear and prompts us to handle them safely.

And, to enable this feature, we need to add the following line inside the **`<PropertyGroup>`** of the projct file:

```
<Nullable>enable</Nullable>
```

The file will now look like:

```
<PropertyGroup>
  <OutputType>Exe</OutputType>
  <TargetFramework>net9.0</TargetFramework>
  <Nullable>enable</Nullable>
</PropertyGroup>
```

This simple change means C# will start warning us if we forget to check for possible nulls in our code.

Updating TaskItem Class for Nullability

Now, we will update the **TaskItem** class so its members clearly reflect whether they can be null. Our title should never be null, but due date can be. Following is the improved version:

```
public class TaskItem
{
    public int Id { get; set; }
    public string Title { get; set; } // Non-nullable
    public bool IsCompleted { get; set; }
    public string? DueDate { get; set; } // Nullable
    public TaskItem(int id, string title, string? dueDate)
    {
        Id = id;
        Title = title;
        DueDate = dueDate;
        IsCompleted = false;
    }
}
```

Now, if we try to assign null to **Title**, or forget to check if a value is null before using it, C# will alert us at compile time. This habit helps prevent a class of bugs that can be difficult to track down later.

Applying Simple Validation during Task Creation

The validation keeps bad data out of our system. When a user creates a new task, we want to make sure the title is not empty or just spaces. This stops us from storing meaningless or unusable tasks.

Given below is a practical way to add validation to the **AddTask** method:

```
static void AddTask()
{
    Console.Write("Enter task title: ");
    string? title = Console.ReadLine();
    // Validation: Title cannot be null or whitespace
    if (string.IsNullOrWhiteSpace(title))
    {
        Console.WriteLine("Task title is required and cannot
be empty.");
        return;
    }
    Console.Write("Enter due date (optional): ");
    string? dueDate = Console.ReadLine();
    if (dueDate != null && dueDate.Trim().Length == 0)
    {
        dueDate = null; // Treat empty input as no due date
    }
    TaskItem newTask = new TaskItem(nextId, title.Trim(),
dueDate);
    tasks.Add(newTask);
    Console.WriteLine($"Task added with Id {nextId}.");
    nextId++;
}
```

In the above, the code checks if the title is missing or just spaces, and if so, informs the user and exits the method early. If the user presses Enter for due date, it is stored as **`null`**.

This makes our application more robust and prevents empty or broken tasks from entering the list.

Handling Bad User Input

We know that validation is not just for task creation. Whenever the program asks for input that must be a number (like a task Id), we should make sure the input is a valid integer and matches an existing task.

For example, the **`CompleteTask`** method already checks for valid integer input, but we can make it clearer:

```
static void CompleteTask()
{
    Console.Write("Enter Id of task to mark as complete: ");
    string? input = Console.ReadLine();
    if (!int.TryParse(input, out int id))
    {
        Console.WriteLine("Please enter a valid number for the task Id.");
        return;
    }
    var task = tasks.Find(t => t.Id == id);
    if (task == null)
    {
        Console.WriteLine("No task found with that Id.");
        return;
    }
    if (task.IsCompleted)
    {
        Console.WriteLine("Task is already completed.");
        return;
    }
```

```
    task.IsCompleted = true;
    Console.WriteLine("Task marked as completed.");
}
```

Now, any invalid or missing input is caught before it causes trouble.

With nullable reference types enabled, all user input validated, and errors handled up front, we avoid the classic pitfalls that trip up many applications. That way, our code becomes more predictable, easier to maintain, and much less likely to crash from null reference exceptions or bad data. These habits are going to be super important when we move on to more complex projects in ASP.NET Core and EF Core, where data from a bunch of users and sources can be unpredictable.

Collections and LINQ Queries

Now that Trackr stores tasks in a list, we can do more than simply add, complete, or show all tasks. The C# provides us with powerful tools through ***LINQ*** (Language Integrated Query) that let us filter, search, and sort collections in a style like SQL, but directly in our code. In this topic, we will learn using LINQ for querying much larger datasets when we move to databases with Entity Framework Core.

Reviewing In-Memory Task List

We are already using a **`List<TaskItem>`** to hold all tasks in memory:

```
static List<TaskItem> tasks = new List<TaskItem>();
```

The **`List`** type is part of the **`System.Collections.Generic`** namespace and acts like a dynamic array, fast to search, easy to grow, and perfect for learning core data management before working with a database.

Filtering Tasks using LINQ

Let us assume that we want to see only tasks that are still pending or only the tasks already completed. The LINQ lets us filter easily using the **`Where`** method.

In the following example, we can show all completed tasks:

```
using System.Linq; // Add this at the top of Program.cs
static void ListCompletedTasks()
{
```

```
    var completedTasks = tasks.Where(t => t.IsCompleted);
    Console.WriteLine("=== Completed Tasks ===");
    foreach (var task in completedTasks)
    {
        string due = task.DueDate ?? "No due date";
        Console.WriteLine($"Id: {task.Id}, Title:
{task.Title}, Due: {due}");
    }
}
```

For pending tasks, we just reverse the check:

```
static void ListPendingTasks()
{
    var pendingTasks = tasks.Where(t => !t.IsCompleted);
    Console.WriteLine("=== Pending Tasks ===");
    foreach (var task in pendingTasks)
    {
        string due = task.DueDate ?? "No due date";
        Console.WriteLine($"Id: {task.Id}, Title:
{task.Title}, Due: {due}");
    }
}
```

These methods help us to see just the tasks we care about. It makes easier to focus and act.

Searching Tasks

Many times, we want to search for tasks containing a certain word or phrase. LINQ's **Where** method works perfectly for this:

```
static void SearchTasks()
{
    Console.Write("Enter keyword to search in task titles: ");
```

```
    string? keyword = Console.ReadLine();
    if (string.IsNullOrWhiteSpace(keyword))
    {
        Console.WriteLine("No keyword entered.");
        return;
    }
    var results = tasks.Where(t =>
        t.Title != null &&
        t.Title.IndexOf(keyword,
StringComparison.OrdinalIgnoreCase) >= 0);
    Console.WriteLine($"=== Tasks containing \"{keyword}\"
===");
    foreach (var task in results)
    {
        string status = task.IsCompleted ? "Completed" :
"Pending";
        string due = task.DueDate ?? "No due date";
        Console.WriteLine($"Id: {task.Id}, Title:
{task.Title}, Status: {status}, Due: {due}");
    }
}
```

This lets we find any task that matches part of the entered text, regardless of case.

Sorting Tasks

When tasks have deadlines, it is helpful to view them in order of due date. LINQ makes sorting easy with the **`OrderBy`** method.

Following is how we can sort tasks (pending ones, for example) by due date:

```
static void ListPendingTasksSortedByDueDate()
{
    var sortedPending = tasks
        .Where(t => !t.IsCompleted && t.DueDate != null)
```

```
        .OrderBy(t => t.DueDate);
    Console.WriteLine("=== Pending Tasks Sorted by Due Date
===");
    foreach (var task in sortedPending)
    {
        string due = task.DueDate ?? "No due date";
        Console.WriteLine($"Id: {task.Id}, Title:
{task.Title}, Due: {due}");
    }
}
```

We can also sort all tasks, including those with no due date, by using **OrderBy** and then **ThenBy**:

```
var sortedAll = tasks
    .OrderBy(t => t.DueDate == null)  // Place tasks with no
due date last
    .ThenBy(t => t.DueDate);
```

Connecting LINQ Features to Menu

We can simply expand the menu in **Main** to include the new features:

```
Console.WriteLine("5. List completed tasks");
Console.WriteLine("6. List pending tasks");
Console.WriteLine("7. Search tasks");
Console.WriteLine("8. List pending tasks sorted by due date");
```

We then add the corresponding cases to the menu switch statement, such that it maps each number to its method.

We then run the application, add several tasks with and without due dates, and then try the new menu options as shown below:

- Option 5 shows only completed tasks.
- Option 6 shows pending tasks.
- Option 7 lets we search by any keyword in the title.

- Option 8 sorts all pending tasks by their due date so we can focus on what needs attention soon.

This should give you the output like the below one:

```
=== Pending Tasks Sorted by Due Date ===
Id: 3, Title: Buy groceries, Due: 2026-01-13
Id: 2, Title: Finish report, Due: 2026-01-15
```

or for search:

```
Enter keyword to search in task titles: report
=== Tasks containing "report" ===
Id: 2, Title: Finish report, Status: Pending, Due: 2026-01-15
```

The more you know about LINQ and in-memory lists, the more confident you'll be when it's time to use databases and EF Core. Almost every business app has filtering, searching, and sorting, and LINQ helps us write clean, readable code for each task. As we keep developing Trackr, LINQ will be our go-to for working with collections and data.

Refactoring Console Logic into Methods and Classes

Until now, we have written most of Trackr's logic directly in the **`Main`** method. This approach is common for small demos, but with the rise of the app, it quickly becomes hard to manage. The large blocks of code in **`Main`** make testing, maintenance, and future changes difficult. In professional development, it is important to break code into logical methods and classes, so each part of the system has a clear responsibility. Hence, if we do refactor the code now itself, we can get the Trackr capable for easier expansion, improved readability, and future features like dependency injection.

Moving Menu Logic into ShowMenu Method

To start with, we will first pull the menu display out of the loop and place it in its own method. This keeps **`Main`** focused on the application's flow and makes the menu easy to adjust or improve.

We then add this method to the **`Program`** class:

```
static void ShowMenu()
{
```

```
    Console.WriteLine();
    Console.WriteLine("==== Trackr Menu ====");
    Console.WriteLine("1. List tasks");
    Console.WriteLine("2. Add task");
    Console.WriteLine("3. Complete task");
    Console.WriteLine("4. Exit");
    Console.Write("Choose an option: ");
}
```

After this, we then update the loop in **Main** to call **ShowMenu()** before reading user input:

```
while (running)
{
    ShowMenu();
    string input = Console.ReadLine();
    // ... (menu handling)
}
```

Extracting Input Handling to Separate Methods

Now here, rather than mixing all logic in the menu's switch statement, we will delegate each action to its own method. It results in **Main** reading almost like a table of contents for the app.

For example, we can refactor the menu switch to:

```
switch (input)
{
    case "1":
        HandleListTasks();
        break;
    case "2":
        HandleCreateTask();
        break;
    case "3":
```

```
        HandleCompleteTask();
        break;
    case "4":
        running = false;
        break;
    default:
        Console.WriteLine("Please choose a valid option.");
        break;
}
```

We can then write methods like:

```
static void HandleListTasks()
{
    TaskService.ListTasks();
}
static void HandleCreateTask()
{
    TaskService.AddTask();
}
static void HandleCompleteTask()
{
    TaskService.CompleteTask();
}
```

Introducing TaskService Class

With the main program now delegating, the next step is to create a separate **TaskService** class. This class will handle all task-related logic, allowing the **Program** class to focus on user interaction.

After this, we will then create a new file named **TaskService.cs** and write:

```
using System;
```

```
using System.Collections.Generic;
public static class TaskService
{
    private static List<TaskItem> tasks = new
List<TaskItem>();
    private static int nextId = 1;
    public static void ListTasks()
    {
        if (tasks.Count == 0)
        {
            Console.WriteLine("No tasks found.");
            return;
        }
        foreach (var task in tasks)
        {
            string status = task.IsCompleted ? "Completed" :
"Pending";
            string due = task.DueDate ?? "No due date";
            Console.WriteLine($"Id: {task.Id}, Title:
{task.Title}, Status: {status}, Due: {due}");
        }
    }
    public static void AddTask()
    {
        Console.Write("Enter task title: ");
        string? title = Console.ReadLine();
        if (string.IsNullOrWhiteSpace(title))
        {
            Console.WriteLine("Task title is required.");
            return;
```

```
        }
        Console.Write("Enter due date (optional): ");
        string? dueDate = Console.ReadLine();
        if (dueDate != null && dueDate.Trim().Length == 0)
        {
            dueDate = null;
        }
        TaskItem newTask = new TaskItem(nextId, title.Trim(),
dueDate);
        tasks.Add(newTask);
        Console.WriteLine($"Task added with Id {nextId}.");
        nextId++;
    }
    public static void CompleteTask()
    {
        Console.Write("Enter Id of task to mark as complete:
");
        string? input = Console.ReadLine();
        if (!int.TryParse(input, out int id))
        {
            Console.WriteLine("Please enter a valid number.");
            return;
        }
        var task = tasks.Find(t => t.Id == id);
        if (task == null)
        {
            Console.WriteLine("No task found with that Id.");
            return;
        }
        if (task.IsCompleted)
```

```
        {
            Console.WriteLine("Task is already completed.");
            return;
        }
        task.IsCompleted = true;
        Console.WriteLine("Task marked as completed.");
    }
}
```

From the above, the entire responsibility for storing, validating, and updating tasks sits in one logical class. All the methods that deal with tasks live in **`TaskService`** which makes the app's design much cleaner.

Final Refactored Program.cs

After all this, the **`Program.cs`** will look streamlined:

```
class Program
{
    static void Main(string[] args)
    {
        bool running = true;
        while (running)
        {
            ShowMenu();
            string input = Console.ReadLine();
            switch (input)
            {
                case "1":
                    HandleListTasks();
                    break;
                case "2":
                    HandleCreateTask();
```

```
                    break;
                case "3":
                    HandleCompleteTask();
                    break;
                case "4":
                    running = false;
                    break;
                default:
                    Console.WriteLine("Please choose a valid
option.");
                    break;
            }
        }
    }
    static void ShowMenu()
    {
        Console.WriteLine();
        Console.WriteLine("==== Trackr Menu ====");
        Console.WriteLine("1. List tasks");
        Console.WriteLine("2. Add task");
        Console.WriteLine("3. Complete task");
        Console.WriteLine("4. Exit");
        Console.Write("Choose an option: ");
    }
    static void HandleListTasks() => TaskService.ListTasks();
    static void HandleCreateTask() => TaskService.AddTask();
    static void HandleCompleteTask() =>
TaskService.CompleteTask();
}
```

This whole approach separates the concern. The **Program** class manages user interaction and flow, while **TaskService** manages data and business logic. Adding new features, like searching or deleting tasks, now means expanding only the **TaskService** and updating the menu. This clean structure sets the foundation for better and advanced organization with the help of dependency injection and interfaces in the future, as we move into web APIs and layered architecture.

Summary

To sum it up, we figured out to build a real console application. We started from the basics of program flow and gradually moved toward a more robust, maintainable structure. We learned how to create an interactive menu using the Main method and explored how to gather and validate user input, using loops and branching statements to control the experience. We then used a simple TaskItem class to model our task data, storing all items in a list and providing clear methods for adding, listing, and marking tasks as complete. With LINQ, we explored some pretty cool ways to filter, search, and sort our collection of tasks in memory, building habits that translate well to database work.

We finally took a look at our code and made some changes. We moved the responsibilities into clear methods and created a TaskService class. This showed us the value of separation of concerns. It also got our codebase ready for growth and testing in the future. This chapter taught us to be methodical and practical when building apps that are easy to maintain, which is key for larger and more complex projects down the road.

CHAPTER 3: DEBUGGING AND TROUBLESHOOTING .NET 9 CODE

Overview

Let's start the next chapter. In this chapter, we're going to focus on building strong debugging and troubleshooting skills. We'll learn to attach the debugger to our Trackr application and place breakpoints to pause execution at meaningful points. I'll go through the code line by line so we can understand how the logic works and how control moves between methods. We'll dive into the call stack to see how it's used to trace execution paths and understand how different layers of code interact. We'll look at how to check variable values using Locals, Autos, and Watch windows, and how to evaluate expressions while paused so we can check assumptions against real runtime data.

Next, we'll dive into understanding exceptions, where we'll purposely cause failures, let them come to the surface, and decode stack traces to quickly find the source of errors in the code. And we'll also talk about logging as a diagnostic tool, showing how to record important events and failures so you can see how the application behaves even without a debugger. And finally, we'll put all these skills to the test by fixing a bug that we'll insert at the start of the process. We'll follow a clear troubleshooting workflow that mirrors real development work.

Attaching Debugger and Stepping Logic

As we keep working on Trackr, our task management console app, it's more and more important to be able to quickly spot and fix mistakes. You know, debugging is one of the most essential skills for any developer. And .NET 9, when paired with Visual Studio Code, offers a powerful yet approachable debugging workflow. We'll be focusing on the hands-on experience of setting breakpoints, launching the debugger, stepping through our code, and using the call stack window to understand how logic flows during typical operations. If we can get a handle on these skills, we'll be able to make troubleshooting a breeze and catch those pesky logic errors way before they end up reaching users.

Placing Breakpoints

A breakpoint is a marker we set on a line of code that tells the debugger to pause execution at that point. This gives us a chance to inspect variables, evaluate expressions, and walk through the application one step at a time.

To place a breakpoint:

1. Open the Trackr solution folder in VS Code.
2. In the Explorer sidebar, expand the files and open **`Program.cs`** or **`TaskService.cs`**.
3. Click to the left of any line number where we want execution to pause, usually on a line inside a method like **`AddTask`**, **`CompleteTask`**, or at the start of our menu loop. A

red dot will appear, showing the breakpoint is set.

For example, placing a breakpoint on the first line of **TaskService.AddTask()**:

```
public static void AddTask()
{
    Console.Write("Enter task title: ");
    // ... rest of method
}
```

This allows us to observe exactly what happens as a user adds a new task, seeing the flow of input, validation, and state changes. We can set as many breakpoints as we like. They can be toggled on or off with a single click, and are visible briefly throughout our codebase.

Starting Debugging Session

Now that we have breakpoints, we can go ahead with launching the debugger. For this:

1. Press **F5** in VS Code, or click the green "Run and Debug" arrow on the sidebar.
2. The first time we do this, VS Code will prompt to select the environment, choose ***.NET 9 (C#)***.

The app will compile and launch in debug mode. The integrated terminal at the bottom of the window acts just like our normal the terminal session, but the debugger is now attached in the background. As soon as execution reaches a line with a breakpoint, the program will pause. The VS Code will highlight the line in yellow and shift the UI to display local variables, call stack, and other debugging panels. We can then observe the state of variables, read the values entered by the user, and inspect how logic flows in detail.

Stepping Into and Over Methods

Once paused at a breakpoint, there are several navigation options that become available:

- ***Step Over (F10):*** This command tells the debugger to execute the current line and move to the next, without diving into any method calls. It is ideal for progressing through a method line by line while keeping the focus local.
- ***Step Into (F11):*** If the current line calls another method, Step Into moves execution into that method, pausing at its first line. This is perfect to analyze how other methods (for example, **TaskService.AddTask**) work from the inside.
- ***Step Out (Shift+F11):*** This command completes execution of the current method and returns to the caller, useful for skipping over large or well-understood code blocks.

Let us say we break at the first line of **AddTask**. By stepping over, we move through each instruction, prompting the user, reading input, performing validation, and adding the task to the list. At any moment, we can hover over variables to see their current value, or look in the "Variables" panel to assess the entire local scope.

If we want to follow the flow from **Program.HandleCreateTask()** into **TaskService.AddTask()**, we use Step Into. This reveals exactly how control moves from the menu handler into the logic that manages tasks, showing each operation along the way.

By combining these navigation options, we can analyze simple errors or complex bugs, catching mistakes before they cause issues downstream.

Experiencing Call Stack Window

When the debugger pauses, the ***Call Stack*** panel on the left of VS Code displays a list of methods that were called to reach the current execution point. Each entry shows the file and line number, letting us trace the complete path the code took.

For example, if we started by choosing "Add Task" in the menu, the call stack might look like:

```
AddTask()          TaskService.cs:45
HandleCreateTask()   Program.cs:67
Main()             Program.cs:22
```

This stack shows that **Main** called **HandleCreateTask**, which called **AddTask**, and that the debugger is currently paused inside **AddTask**. Hence, by clicking any item in the call stack, we can instantly navigate to that method's source code, reviewing how values were passed along the way.

Inspecting and Modifying Variables

While debugging, we can do more than observe. The Variables panel shows every local and global variable at the current breakpoint. We can:

- Expand variables to see their fields and properties.
- Hover over variable names in the editor to see current values.
- Change the value of a variable mid-execution, letting us test hypotheses or simulate conditions (for instance, setting **task.IsCompleted = true** before a check).

If we have a bug where tasks are not being marked as completed, we can pause inside the relevant method and observe the task's properties to understand better where things are going wrong. For example, we might notice that the task was not found, or that the Id was misparsed.

Setting Conditional Breakpoints

To save time in larger apps, we can use ***conditional breakpoints***. For this, we just have to right-click on a breakpoint and add a condition, such as **`id == 5`**, so that the debugger only pauses when that exact value is encountered. This is very helpful if we are only interested in a specific scenario or bug.

The Debug Console at the bottom of VS Code also allows us to evaluate expressions and call methods in the running program. For example, typing **`tasks.Count`** and pressing Enter will print the number of tasks currently in memory. We can use this to quickly inspect or test small pieces of logic.

You may try the following example:

1. We place a breakpoint at the first line of **`AddTask`** in **`TaskService.cs`**.
2. Start debugging with **`F5`**.
3. In the Trackr menu, select the option to add a new task.
4. As soon as **`AddTask`** is called, the debugger pauses.
5. Use ***Step Over*** to walk through input, validation, and adding the task.
6. Observe how **`tasks`** grow by one after adding.
7. Use the Call Stack panel to see how the code moved from **`Main`** to **`HandleCreateTask`** to **`AddTask`**.

If we spot a bug (such as an empty title getting through), we can immediately test a fix, restart debugging, and confirm the result.

When you learn to use breakpoints, stepping, variable inspection, and the call stack, you'll feel more confident finding and fixing bugs early on. This goes from small console applications like Trackr to much larger systems with many layers. This way, we can watch the app's logic unfold step by step, uncovering issues that are hard to find with print statements or guesswork.

Inspecting Variables and Evaluating Expressions

Now that we have learned to pause Trackr at breakpoints and step through logic, the next step is learning to ***inspect variables*** and ***evaluate expressions*** using the built-in windows of VS Code. We will see the current state of our application, and to directly compare our assumptions with what is happening as Trackr runs. FYI, the habit of checking variables at each breakpoint, testing expressions, and verifying our predictions is essential for professional troubleshooting in any real-world project.

Locals, Autos, and Watch

When the Trackr is paused at a breakpoint, there are three key panels in the VS Code Debug pane that come into play:

Locals Window

The ***Locals*** window displays all variables that are in the current scope of the paused line. For example, if we are paused inside the **`AddTask`** method, we will see all local variables, such as **`title`**, **`dueDate`**, and **`newTask`**, as well as parameters to the method. This view automatically updates as we step through the code, always showing only the variables that are active at the current execution point.

To use the Locals window:

- Start debugging and pause at a breakpoint inside any method.
- Expand the "Locals" section in the left sidebar.
- Review the list of variable names, types, and current values.

Autos Window

The ***Autos*** window is a smart list that shows variables the debugger predicts are most relevant, usually those just used or about to be used in the next lines of code. It is particularly useful for quickly checking values involved in the most recent operations, such as user input, loop counters, or return values.

The Autos window is especially helpful when stepping through short, focused methods, giving instant feedback without overwhelming detail.

Watch Window

The ***Watch*** window allows us to specify any variables or expressions we want to keep an eye on, regardless of scope. We can add variable names, properties, or even C# expressions (such as **`tasks.Count`** or **`title.ToUpper()`**) and see their values update live as we step through code.

To use the Watch window:

- In the Debug pane, locate the "Watch" section.
- Click "Add Expression" and enter any variable or expression.
- The value updates automatically whenever that variable is in scope.

This is extremely useful for tracking how a value changes through a method or over the lifetime of an operation.

Inspecting Variable Values while Paused

Here, I will take you through a typical debugging session as below:

1. We first place a breakpoint at the start of **`TaskService.AddTask()`**.
2. Then, we start debugging with **`F5`**.
3. We then choose "Add task" in Trackr's menu.
4. When paused, we will look at the ***Locals*** window to see the initial values of all local variables.
5. After this, we will enter a task title and press Enter. After stepping over the input line, check how the value of **`title`** has changed.

We will continue stepping and observe the values of **`dueDate`** and the new **`TaskItem`** as they are set.

At each step, the Locals and Autos windows let us verify:

- Is the input value what we expected?
- Did the code correctly handle empty or bad input?
- Is the new task created with the right properties?

If a variable is not showing the value we predict, this is often a clue that a bug or misunderstanding exists in the logic.

Evaluating Simple Expressions

Now, let us think that we are tracking an issue where not all tasks are being added as expected. So here, we can use the Watch window to monitor the count of tasks:

- Add **`tasks.Count`** to the Watch window before and after the **`tasks.Add(newTask)`** line.
- Step over the add operation and see if the count increases.

Or, if we want to keep track of the status of the last task, then we can simply add **`tasks.Last().IsCompleted`** as a watched expression. It will allow us to see immediately whether new tasks are set as incomplete, or if something is going wrong with default values.

The routine of inspecting variables and evaluating expressions at every breakpoint becomes a professional habit, setting us up for effective debugging in any .NET 9 application, from console utilities to enterprise APIs.

Understanding Exceptions and Stack Traces

Every developer, no matter how careful, encounters exceptions. Exceptions are .NET's way of saying, "Something happened here that cannot be handled in the normal flow." Rather than feeling frustrated when errors appear, we can use them to learn exactly where, why, and how things went wrong. By intentionally causing exceptions in Trackr, observing the resulting stack traces, and using Visual Studio Code's tools to jump right to the problem lines, we will build the confidence to turn error messages into rapid solutions.

Intentionally Causing Exceptions

To explore exceptions, we can deliberately create a few common error scenarios. For our demonstration, we will focus on two types: ***null reference exceptions*** and ***invalid input exceptions***.

Null Reference Exception

We can create a scenario where our code attempts to access a property or method on a **`null`** object. The following example shows how to do this in the **`TaskService`** class:

```
public static void CauseNullReference()
{
    TaskItem? brokenTask = null;
    // The next line will throw a NullReferenceException
    Console.WriteLine(brokenTask.Title);
}
```

We then add a temporary menu item in the program's menu:

```
Console.WriteLine("5. Cause Null Reference Exception");
```

After this, we then update the switch block:

```
case "5":
    TaskService.CauseNullReference();
    break;
```

Invalid Input Exception

Here, we will force an unhandled exception by parsing non-numeric input as an integer:

```
public static void CauseInvalidInputException()
```

```
{
    Console.Write("Enter a number: ");
    string? input = Console.ReadLine();
    // The next line will throw a FormatException if input is
not a number
    int number = int.Parse(input);
    Console.WriteLine($"You entered: {number}");
}
```

We will add this to the menu as well:

```
Console.WriteLine("6. Cause Invalid Input Exception");
```

And then in the switch:

```
case "6":
    TaskService.CauseInvalidInputException();
    break;
```

Allowing Exceptions to Propagate and Observing Stack Traces

Now, we will run the application in debug mode (**F5**). Here, we will choose either of these new options. For the null reference scenario, as soon as the line tries to print **brokenTask.Title**, the .NET will throw a **NullReferenceException**.

And, what we see in the terminal will look like this:

```
Unhandled exception. System.NullReferenceException: Object
reference not set to an instance of an object.
   at TaskService.CauseNullReference() in
C:\Path\To\TaskService.cs:line 100
   at Program.Main(String[] args) in
C:\Path\To\Program.cs:line 50
```

For invalid input scenario, the non-numeric text like "abc" will throw **FormatException**:

```
Unhandled exception. System.FormatException: Input string was
not in a correct format.
```

```
    at System.Number.ThrowOverflowOrFormatException()
    at System.Int32.Parse(String s)
    at TaskService.CauseInvalidInputException() in
C:\Path\To\TaskService.cs:line 110
    at Program.Main(String[] args) in
C:\Path\To\Program.cs:line 50
```

The stack trace tells us not just that an error occurred, but exactly which lines and methods were involved, from the origin point all the way back up the call stack.

Reading Stack Trace and Jumping to Source Lines

A stack trace is a reverse-chronological record of method calls that led up to the exception. Each entry shows the method, the file, and the line number. For example:

```
at TaskService.CauseNullReference() in
C:\Path\To\TaskService.cs:line 100

at Program.Main(String[] args) in C:\Path\To\Program.cs:line
50
```

In the above, the first line is where the exception actually happened. And, each following line is the method that called it, going up to **Main**.

To jump to source, the stack trace in the terminal will display as clickable links (if using the integrated terminal). Here, we have to click on **TaskService.cs:line 100**, and VS Code opens the file at the exact line where the problem occurred. This workflow then lets us immediately locate and analyze the code responsible for the exception, rather than guessing or hunting through files.

If running outside the debugger, copy the file path and line number from the stack trace and use VS Code's "Go to File" and "Go to Line" features (**Ctrl+P**, then **:100**) to jump directly to the problem.

If we read the stack trace carefully, we can see the order in which methods were called, the parameters passed, and how control flowed. This is invaluable when troubleshooting more complex issues. For example, if the trace points to a utility method deep in our app, we know the full sequence of calls that brought us there, and we can work backward to see what inputs or state might have triggered the exception.

This is exactly how issues are diagnosed and fixed in real production systems.

Adding Basic Logging

Over time, we want to know not only when things succeed, but especially when something goes wrong. The concept of logging helps us answer such questions like:

- When did a task get added or completed?
- Was there a failure when the user tried to mark a task as complete?
- What was the last thing the app did before an error?

With the logging, it prepares ourselves to observe Trackr's behavior outside the debugger.

Configuring Logging with Built-In Abstractions

We begin with wire up the logging using only .NET's built-in libraries. For this, we open our **Program.cs** and add:

```
using Microsoft.Extensions.Logging;
```

In our **Main** method, just above our menu loop, we then set up the logger like this:

```
var loggerFactory = LoggerFactory.Create(builder =>
{
    builder.AddSimpleConsole(options =>
    {
        options.SingleLine = true;
        options.TimestampFormat = "HH:mm:ss ";
    });
    builder.SetMinimumLevel(LogLevel.Information);
});
ILogger logger = loggerFactory.CreateLogger("Trackr");
```

With this, we now have a logger ready to record information, warnings, and errors, each with a timestamp and clear format.

Passing Logger to TaskService

The Trackr's logic mostly lives inside **TaskService**. To connect our logger, we then shall update the **TaskService**:

For this, we will add a static field for the logger:

```
private static ILogger? _logger;
```

Then, we add a method to assign the logger when Trackr starts:

```
public static void SetLogger(ILogger logger)
{
    _logger = logger;
}
```

In **Program.cs**, just after creating the logger, we then set it for **TaskService**:

```
TaskService.SetLogger(logger);
```

This lets every action in Trackr write log entries, making diagnostics possible.

Logging Key Actions

We will log whenever something important happens, like creating or completing a task, and log warnings or errors for failed operations. So here, we will update the **AddTask** and **CompleteTask**:

- Logging Task Creation

```
public static void AddTask()
{
    Console.Write("Enter task title: ");
    string? title = Console.ReadLine();
    if (string.IsNullOrWhiteSpace(title))
    {
        _logger?.LogWarning("Attempted to create a task with
an empty title.");
        Console.WriteLine("Task title is required.");
        return;
    }
    Console.Write("Enter due date (optional): ");
    string? dueDate = Console.ReadLine();
```

```
    if (dueDate != null && dueDate.Trim().Length == 0)
    {
        dueDate = null;
    }
    TaskItem newTask = new TaskItem(nextId, title.Trim(),
dueDate);
    tasks.Add(newTask);
    _logger?.LogInformation("Task created. Id={Id},
Title={Title}", newTask.Id, newTask.Title);
    Console.WriteLine($"Task added with Id {nextId}.");
    nextId++;
}
```

- Logging Task Completion and Failures

```
public static void CompleteTask()
{
    Console.Write("Enter Id of task to mark as complete: ");
    string? input = Console.ReadLine();
    if (!int.TryParse(input, out int id))
    {
        _logger?.LogWarning("User entered invalid Id format:
{Input}", input);
        Console.WriteLine("Please enter a valid number.");
        return;
    }
    var task = tasks.Find(t => t.Id == id);
    if (task == null)
    {
        _logger?.LogWarning("No task found for Id={Id} during
completion attempt.", id);
        Console.WriteLine("No task found with that Id.");
```

```
        return;
    }
    if (task.IsCompleted)
    {
        _logger?.LogInformation("User attempted to complete
already completed task. Id={Id}", id);
        Console.WriteLine("Task is already completed.");
        return;
    }
    task.IsCompleted = true;
    _logger?.LogInformation("Task marked as completed.
Id={Id}", id);
    Console.WriteLine("Task marked as completed.");
}
```

With this, every successful and unsuccessful attempt to add or complete a task will create a clear entry in the logs.

Following is a good example of such a log:

```
16:08:11 [INF] Task created. Id=1, Title=Finish homework
16:08:15 [WRN] Attempted to create a task with an empty title.
16:08:20 [INF] Task marked as completed. Id=1
16:08:25 [WRN] No task found for Id=5 during completion
attempt.
```

These logs are our application's "memory" of what happened, providing us with insights even if we missed something in the UI.

As we grow more comfortable with logging, we learn to use logs for troubleshooting when users report problems, or when behavior is not as expected. The inclusion of enough information (Id, Title, user input, etc.) in each message helps us to retrace steps, confirm the sequence of events, and diagnose subtle bugs, even if we are nowhere near the debugger.

Fixing Bug

What really helps a junior developer grow is seeing a bug from start to finish, from discovery to resolution. In this section, we're going to deliberately introduce a minor bug into Trackr, then take it apart step by step to figure out what's causing it and how to fix it. We'll use logging and debugging to do this. This is the kind of troubleshooting workflow that will make us stand out as problem solvers ready for real software projects.

Inserting Subtle Bug

So here, we will first introduce a classic off-by-one error when creating new tasks. The intention is for every new task to receive a unique Id, but we will make a tiny change that will cause some tasks to be assigned the same Id.

To begin, we will open the **TaskService.AddTask** method and change this line:

```
TaskItem newTask = new TaskItem(nextId, title.Trim(),
dueDate);
tasks.Add(newTask);
_logger?.LogInformation("Task created. Id={Id},
Title={Title}", newTask.Id, newTask.Title);
Console.WriteLine($"Task added with Id {nextId}.");
nextId++;
```

to this buggy version:

```
TaskItem newTask = new TaskItem(nextId, title.Trim(),
dueDate);
tasks.Add(newTask);
_logger?.LogInformation("Task created. Id={Id},
Title={Title}", newTask.Id, newTask.Title);
Console.WriteLine($"Task added with Id {nextId}.");
// BUG: forgot to increment nextId here
// nextId++;
```

In this, we comment out the line that increments **nextId**. As a result, every new task will be created with the same Id.

Reproducing Bug

Next, we now build and run Trackr:

- Add a first task ("Task A"). The app says, "Task added with Id 1."
- Add a second task ("Task B"). Again, "Task added with Id 1."
- Add a third ("Task C"). Still, "Task added with Id 1."

This thing lists the tasks. All of them have Id 1! This makes it impossible to complete or distinguish between tasks correctly. This type of bug is very common, especially as logic changes and small lines are accidentally omitted.

Observing Bug Symptoms using Logging

Next, we then check the log output in the console as we add several tasks. The log will show:

```
16:14:40 [INF] Task created. Id=1, Title=Task A
16:14:48 [INF] Task created. Id=1, Title=Task B
16:14:53 [INF] Task created. Id=1, Title=Task C
```

Here, we notice that all logs report the same Id for different titles. This is our first clue that something is off in task creation logic. When we try to complete a task, it is ambiguous which task is being marked, or multiple completions might affect the same one.

Debugging for Root Cause

Now, we will use VS Code's debugger to track down the problem. And for this, we will:

1. Place a breakpoint at the first line of **`TaskService.AddTask()`**.
2. Start debugging (**`F5`**) and add a task.
3. Step through the method line by line. Watch the value of **`nextId`** in the Locals or Watch window. After adding a task, check: did **`nextId`** increase?
4. Step again to add another task. Observe that **`nextId`** never changes, so every new task gets the same Id.

If we are unsure where **`nextId`** is used, we can right-click **`nextId`** and "Find All References" in VS Code to see where we should be incrementing it.

Fixing Bug and Verifying Solution

Once we realize the **`nextId`** is not being incremented, we then re-enable the line:

```
nextId++;
```

Now, we will rerun the app:

- Add three tasks.
- Each gets Id 1, then 2, then 3, both in logs and in the displayed list.

The logs will now read as below:

```
16:17:01 [INF] Task created. Id=1, Title=Task A
16:17:09 [INF] Task created. Id=2, Title=Task B
16:17:15 [INF] Task created. Id=3, Title=Task C
```

With this, the completing and listing of tasks now works correctly, as each one is uniquely identified.

This end-to-end troubleshooting not only builds confidence but also prepares us for the challenges of real software development, where logging and debugging together let us move from "something is wrong" to "here is exactly how to fix it".

Summary

Basically, we figured out how to systematically debug and troubleshoot .NET 9 applications using practical, tool-driven techniques. We practiced using the debugger with our Trackr console app and setting breakpoints to pause execution at important points. We used the step into and step over actions to figure out how control moved across methods. We checked out the call stack to see how execution went from the Main method into handlers and service methods, which helped us figure out layered logic. We checked the values using Locals, Autos, and Watch windows, and evaluated expressions while paused to compare our expectations with the actual runtime state. We intentionally triggered exceptions, let them spread, and learned to read stack traces to figure out exactly which source file and line number was causing the problems. We practiced navigating directly from stack frames back to code, which made us feel more confident when decoding error output. We then started using structured logging with built-in logging abstractions to capture task creation, updates, and failures.

We finally did a full troubleshooting cycle, which included inserting a small bug, reproducing it, diagnosing it through logs and debugging tools, fixing the issue, and validating the fix. This chapter really reinforced our problem-solving mindset and got us ready to handle failures with clarity and discipline.

CHAPTER 4: WORKING WITH EXISTING .NET APPLICATIONS

Overview

So in this chapter, we're going to learn how to work effectively with existing .NET applications, even when we're joining a project for the first time. We'll open a prebuilt solution and use Visual Studio Code's navigation tools to explore its projects, folders, and files, building a mental map of the system's structure. We'll learn to map components to their responsibilities, understand unfamiliar naming patterns and architectural choices. We'll be practicing reproducing and diagnosing known bugs, triggering them step by step, and enhancing the code with targeted logs and checks to capture the exact conditions under which failures occur.

This chapter will teach us how to follow a request from the user interface or entry point, through service and business logic, down to data access. We'll use breakpoints and variable inspection to trace values and behavior across all layers. We'll also learn how to safely apply small refactorings, extracting methods, introducing helper classes, and renaming unclear identifiers, so the codebase becomes more readable and maintainable without changing its logic. And when we've got those techniques down, we'll be able to jump in and help out on any existing .NET project, turning unfamiliar systems into chances to figure out what's going on, make improvements safely, and put our software skills to work.

Navigating Unknown Codebase

When developers join a new team or are handed a prebuilt .NET solution, that's usually one of the most common real-world experiences they have. When you see folders, files, and code you're not familiar with, it can be a bit shocking at first. The key to getting past this isn't just memorization. It's using proven methods and tools to map out the code base, understand its components, and feel confident jumping between related parts. In this topic, we're going to take a peek at a small prebuilt .NET solution, check out its structure, and use Visual Studio Code to jump around quickly between definitions, references, and call sites.

Scanning Prebuilt .NET Solution

To begin with, we will consider that we have received a zipped folder containing a .NET solution. The following steps is what the approach we will adhere to:

Open Solution

- Unzip the folder and open Visual Studio Code.
- Choose ***File > Open Folder…*** and select the root of the prebuilt solution. The Solution Explorer will display all the files and subfolders.

Recognize Main Components

At the top level, we will typically see a file ending in **`.sln`** (the solution file) and several subfolders, each representing a project (for example, **`Api`**, **`Core`**, **`Web`**, **`Data`**, or **`Tests`**). Every project usually contains a **`.csproj`** file (the project file).

After this, we will then look for the following typical folders:

- ***Controllers*** or ***Api***: Entry points for HTTP requests (if web API)
- ***Models*** or ***Entities***: Data definitions
- ***Services*** or ***Logic***: Business rules and operations
- ***Data*** or ***Repositories***: Data access code
- ***Views***: UI files (for MVC or desktop apps)
- ***Tests***: Unit or integration tests

We are not required to read every file, as we are looking to spot the neighborhoods of the codebase.

Mapping Projects to Responsibilities

In almost every multi-project solution, each project usually serves a focused purpose. So here, we will map some typical names to roles:

- ***Solution.sln*** is the umbrella file, linking all projects.
- ***MyApp.Api*** handles incoming requests, defines API endpoints.
- ***MyApp.Core*** contains business logic, interfaces, and domain models.
- ***MyApp.Data*** contains data access, Entity Framework migrations, repositories.
- ***MyApp.Web*** is the Web UI, And
- ***MyApp.Tests*** contains all test code.

Exploring Folders and File Responsibilities

Next, within each project, we will then break down folders:

- ***Controllers*** represents an endpoint. For example, **`TaskController.cs`** will manage HTTP requests for tasks.
- ***Models*** or ***Entities*** contains data structures. For example, **`TaskItem.cs`** defines the properties and types for a task.
- ***Services*** folder contain business logic, orchestrate workflows, like **`TaskService.cs`** encapsulates task creation, updating, and validation.
- ***Repositories*** contains classes that talk to databases or other storage.
- ***Utils*** contains utility functions used throughout the app.

Definitions, References, and Call Sites

To understand a codebase, you need to follow the logic flow. Thankfully, VS Code gives us shortcuts for this.

Go to Definition

Here, just places the cursor on any type, method, or variable. Then, press **F12** (or right-click and choose "Go to Definition"). The VS Code jumps directly to where the method, class, or property is declared, even across projects.

For example, if we see **TaskService.CreateTask()**, then just press **F12** on **CreateTask** to see its implementation in the service layer.

Peek Definition

For this, press **Alt+F12** to see the implementation in a popup, so we do not lose the current place.

Find All References

To do this, place the cursor on a class, method, or property. Then press **Shift+F12** (or right-click and choose "Find All References"). After this, the VS Code will list every location where the symbol is used.

This is invaluable for tracking down all uses of a model or service and mapping call sites.

Go to Implementation

For interfaces or virtual methods, we can just press **Ctrl+F12** to jump to concrete implementations.

This makes tracing abstraction boundaries straightforward.

Mapping Components to Responsibilities

Now here, imagine, we have spotted **TaskController.cs**. And inside it, we can see a method like:

```
public IActionResult Create(TaskItemDto task)
{
    return _taskService.CreateTask(task);
}
```

So here, we will use ***Go to Definition*** on **_taskService** or **CreateTask** to jump to the business logic.

Now, in **`TaskService.cs`**, see what happens when a task is created. Then, try to find the references to **`TaskItemDto`** to understand its structure and usage. If **`CreateTask`** calls a repository, follow the flow with ***Go to Definition*** again.

You need to repeat this workflow to follow a request or operation from the API/controller, through services, down to data, and back.

Fast Exploration

Sometimes, the following helps to see all mentions of a word or type across the solution:

- Press **`Ctrl+Shift+F`** to search for any text (for example, "TaskItem").
- Filter results by file type or folder.
- Use "Go to File" (**`Ctrl+P`**) to jump quickly when we know the file name.

If we are looking for application entry points, search for **`Main`** or for **`[HttpGet]`**, **`[HttpPost]`**, etc., to see which controllers respond to HTTP requests.

Application Mental Model

After a short period of navigating with these tools:

- You will recognize where the application starts and how a request flows through.
- You will map business logic to services, data access to repositories, and understand where models are defined and transformed.
- You will be able to trace a feature from UI or API endpoint, through service and repository, down to the database or storage.

Do not worry if every detail is not clear at first. The more we jump between definitions, references, and call sites, the more the codebase's "shape" will emerge.

This approach prepares us to join any .NET project, open the solution, and make sense of its layout. We will no longer feel lost when handed an unfamiliar codebase.

Reproducing and Logging Existing Bugs

No matter how well a .NET application is built, bugs inevitably surface, sometimes after months of real-world use. The real skill is not just fixing bugs, but learning to reproduce them reliably, observe their conditions, and collect evidence with targeted logging and assertions. This approach transforms every bug from a mystery into a step-by-step workflow.

So here, we will take the prebuilt .NET solution we explored previously, and then we will find a known defect, trigger it on purpose, and then will try to improve our diagnostic skills by adding logs and assertions.

Identifying Bug

Suppose that in our app, there is a known defect which is when adding a new Task, it leaves the title empty, and thereby it causes the application to crash instead of displaying an error.

So here, we will try to trigger this bug on demand so we can observe its context, gather useful logs, and assert the right expectations.

Reproducing Bug

Find Feature in Codebase

We will first open the project and use the file tree or search (**`Ctrl+P`** or **`Ctrl+Shift+F`**) to find the code responsible for task creation.

And let us say that we located **`TaskService.AddTask()`**.

Trigger the Bug

Now, we will start the app, go to the UI to add a task. At the prompt for task title, you then press 'Enter' without typing anything.

Now here, instead of a validation message, the application crashes with an exception (such as a **`NullReferenceException`** or similar).

This step proves the bug is reproducible and not just a rumor.

Adding Targeted Logs and Assertions

To diagnose and ultimately fix the bug, we will then log key actions and add an assertion (or explicit check) to catch the problem early.

Adding Targeted Logs

We will go to the method where the bug occurs, for example:

```
public static void AddTask()
{
    // Add a log entry before validation
    _logger?.LogInformation("Attempting to add a new task.
Input received.");
    Console.Write("Enter task title: ");
```

```
    string? title = Console.ReadLine();
    _logger?.LogInformation("Task title received: {Title}",
title);
    // The bug is that we do not validate for empty or null
title
    // Adding a log for validation
    if (string.IsNullOrWhiteSpace(title))
    {
        _logger?.LogWarning("Task title was empty or
whitespace. Aborting creation.");
        Console.WriteLine("Task title cannot be empty.");
        return;
    }
    // Continue as before
    // ...
}
```

Adding Assertion

In .NET console applications, we often use early returns rather than formal assertions, but it prevent the code from running if expectations are not met.

```
if (string.IsNullOrWhiteSpace(title))
{
    _logger?.LogWarning("Task creation aborted due to empty
title.");
    Console.WriteLine("Task title is required.");
    return;
}
```

If the application is meant to be used in testing scenarios or larger codebases, we could also add assertions with **`Debug.Assert()`** from the **`System.Diagnostics`** namespace, but logging and early checks work well in most practical cases.

Observing Bug with Enabled Logs

Now, we will repeat the earlier steps, like starting the app, and triggering the bug by leaving the title empty.

Now here, instead of crashing, we will now see:

```
Attempting to add a new task. Input received.
Task title received:
Task title was empty or whitespace. Aborting creation.
Task title cannot be empty.
```

And, if logging to a file or the console, the log captures a timestamped record of the error and input. This is necessary for troubleshooting after deployment, when interactive debugging is not available.

From now on, when a bug is reported, we just have to adopt the following workflow:

1. ***Reproduce***: Trigger the bug based on user description or known scenario.
2. ***Observe***: Note exact symptoms, error messages, and code paths.
3. ***Instrument***: Add logs before, during, and after suspected problem areas.
4. ***Assert***: Add validation checks to guard against bad states.
5. ***Retest***: Try to reproduce again, if the bug is stopped early or logs reveal the culprit, we have a clear fix or a solid trail for further assessment.

This is quite a systematic approach, and it takes fear out of legacy or unfamiliar code and builds a toolkit for confident, repeatable bug diagnosis.

Debugging across Layers (UI, API, and Data)

Most of the modern .NET applications rarely exist as a single file or project. The solutions are generally layered, splitting responsibilities across user interface, service (business) logic, and data access code. The bugs can surface in any of these layers, or even due to the way they interact. If we carry the ability to debug across these boundaries, following a request from UI to API to data and back, then only we can determine how effectively we solve real, production issues.

So here, in this topic, we will explore to attach the debugger and practically trace a feature end-to-end, inspecting state at each layer.

Attaching Debugger

We will first open our multi-project .NET solution in Visual Studio Code. For a web API, we will ensure the launch configuration is set up to start the project we want to debug. If we are dealing with a desktop app, we will then start with the UI project.

Just follow the below steps:

- In VS Code, select the Run and Debug icon.
- Choose the right launch profile (for example, ".NET Core Launch (web)" for a Web API or ".NET Core Launch (console)" for desktop).
- Press **`F5`** to launch in debug mode.

The debugger attaches automatically, and breakpoints anywhere in the codebase will be respected, no matter which project owns them.

Following Request

Now suppose the application allows a user to create a new task via the UI, which calls the API, which then stores the task in a database.

For this, we will practice the following operation step by step:

Place Breakpoints in each Layer

In UI Layer, we place a breakpoint on the code that fires when the user submits the "Add Task" form or clicks "Create Task."

In API/Service Layer, we then place a breakpoint in the method that receives the API call and invokes business logic (for example, **`TaskController.Create`** or **`TaskService.CreateTask`**).

And finally in Data Layer, we will place a breakpoint in the method that saves or queries the task in the database, such as a repository's **`Add`** or **`SaveChanges`** method.

Initiate Operation from UI

- Launch the UI as usual.
- And then fill out the "Add Task" form and submit.

As soon as execution hits the first breakpoint, the debugger will pause.

Inspecting State at Boundary

At UI Layer

- Assess the input fields, does the data match what the user entered?
- Is the request payload correct (for web: look at form or JSON data; for desktop: assess in-memory object)?

We will continue to let execution flow to the next breakpoint.

At Service Layer

- Check if the request object arrived correctly.
- Are any fields missing or incorrectly mapped?
- Is the business logic validating or transforming the input as expected?

We can add expressions like **`task.Title`** or **`ModelState.IsValid`** to the Watch window to confirm expectations.

After this, we will then continue to move into the data layer.

At Data Layer

- Inspect the entity about to be saved.
- Check if fields are set as expected (for example, **`DueDate`**, **`IsCompleted`**).
- In the case of Entity Framework, we can inspect the change tracker or SQL command generated.
- Confirm that **`dbContext.SaveChanges()`** or the repository method will store the correct state.

Diagnosing Layers Issues

Now here, let us consider that the task does not appear in the UI after creation. So here, we now step backward:

- Did the data layer receive the right values?
- Did the API/service transform or validate data incorrectly?
- Did the UI send an incomplete or malformed request?

We will pause and inspect at each boundary, such that we can pinpoint exactly where the data stopped matching our expectations. For even deeper diagnostics, we can combine this process with targeted logging.

So here, we will now add log entries at entry and exit points of each layer:

```
_logger?.LogInformation("UI received input: {Title}, {DueDate}", title, dueDate);

_logger?.LogInformation("API received task: {Title}, {DueDate}", task.Title, task.DueDate);
```

```
_logger?.LogInformation("Data layer saving task: {Title},
{DueDate}", entity.Title, entity.DueDate);
```

The log output then forms a "breadcrumb trail," showing the values as they pass through each part of the app.

While stepping through code, the ***Call Stack*** window in VS Code shows the entire path from UI handler, to API method, to service, and finally to repository or data method. Clicking each entry moves us to the source file and line, so we can see the complete sequence. We can also use the ***Watch*** window to monitor key variables (**`Title`**, **`DueDate`**, **`Id`**) across layers. If the value changes unexpectedly, we will spot exactly where.

At each boundary, we verify state, logic, and transformations. This process, paired with logs, gives us a complete view of how layers interact, empowering us to diagnose even the most complex, cross-layer issues. As we continue, this workflow ensures that multi-layered code never needs to feel intimidating or opaque.

Applying Safe Refactorings in Legacy Code

While working with an existing codebase, especially one that has evolved over time, it is common to spot areas that can be improved for clarity and maintainability, even if the logic is technically correct. The whole concept of refactoring aims at improving the internal structure of code without changing its external behavior. And there are small, focused refactorings that not only make code easier to read and understand, but also help us reduce the chance of bugs creeping in as the project grows.

So here in this topic, we will identify opportunities for extracting methods, introducing helper classes, and renaming identifiers. We will take each step carefully, always confirming that the app's behavior remains unchanged.

Spotting Opportunities for Refactoring

We will first open a file like **`TaskService.cs`** or any area that has grown complicated. There are typical "smells" to look for are:

- Very long methods that try to do too much
- Repeated code blocks (copy-paste or logic that looks nearly identical)
- Variable or method names that are unclear or misleading
- Groups of related functions that could be grouped in a helper class

For example, if we have a method for adding a task that handles user input, validation, and creation all in one place.

Extracting Methods

Now let us consider that the following is our original code:

```
public static void AddTask()
{
    Console.Write("Enter task title: ");
    string? title = Console.ReadLine();
    if (string.IsNullOrWhiteSpace(title))
    {
        Console.WriteLine("Task title is required.");
        return;
    }
    Console.Write("Enter due date (optional): ");
    string? dueDate = Console.ReadLine();
    TaskItem newTask = new TaskItem(nextId, title.Trim(),
dueDate);
    tasks.Add(newTask);
    Console.WriteLine($"Task added with Id {nextId}.");
    nextId++;
}
```

Now here, we will extract the user input and validation logic to their own method:

```
private static string PromptForTitle()
{
    while (true)
    {
        Console.Write("Enter task title: ");
        string? title = Console.ReadLine();
        if (!string.IsNullOrWhiteSpace(title))
            return title.Trim();
```

```
        Console.WriteLine("Task title is required.");
    }
}
```

After this, the **AddTask** becomes cleaner:

```
public static void AddTask()
{
    string title = PromptForTitle();
    Console.Write("Enter due date (optional): ");
    string? dueDate = Console.ReadLine();
    TaskItem newTask = new TaskItem(nextId, title, dueDate);
    tasks.Add(newTask);
    Console.WriteLine($"Task added with Id {nextId}.");
    nextId++;
}
```

This makes future changes and testing easier, if the input prompt changes, we only update one place.

Introducing Helper Classes

If we see a cluster of static functions dealing with date parsing, validation, or formatting, it is often a sign they belong together. For example, let us consider that we want to extract date handling into a helper class:

```
public static class DateHelper
{
    public static string? ParseDueDate(string? input)
    {
        if (string.IsNullOrWhiteSpace(input))
            return null;
        return input.Trim();
    }
```

```
}
```

We then update the main logic to use the helper:

```
string? dueDate = DateHelper.ParseDueDate(Console.ReadLine());
```

Now, every part of the codebase uses a consistent and central approach to dates.

Checking for Behavior Changes

After each small refactoring:

- We will uild and run the application.
- We then test the feature to confirm it still works exactly as before. And,
- If available, we will run the test suite (unit or integration tests) to check for regressions.

If something breaks, we can use undo (**`Ctrl+Z`**) or revert changes and try a smaller, more focused refactor.

The key is to break it down into small steps. We can do this by extracting a single method, introducing one helper class, or renaming a few variables at a time. This keeps the code safe and easy to understand. Every improvement builds confidence for the next change, so over time, the codebase evolves to be easier to work with, even if it started out tangled or confusing.

Summary

As we learned in this chapter, we can now approach, understand, and improve existing .NET applications with confidence and systematic practices. We kicked things off by taking a look at a prebuilt .NET solution, mapping its projects, folders, and components to their responsibilities. We used Visual Studio Code's navigation features to jump between definitions, references, and call sites, quickly getting oriented in a codebase we hadn't seen before.

Then, we focused on reproducing known bugs. We identified a defect, triggered it step by step, and learned to add targeted logs and assertions to capture the precise circumstances of failure. We followed a request from the user interface through the API and into the data layer, attaching the debugger and checking the application's state at each boundary. At last, we used safe, incremental refactorings. This meant taking methods out of long routines, creating helper classes for repeated logic, and renaming identifiers for clarity. After each change, we checked that the app's behavior didn't change. This chapter gave us the skills we need to work with, understand, and improve legacy .NET solutions.

Chapter 5: Revisiting ASP.NET Core and HTTP Basics

Overview

In this new chapter, we're going to learn to connect console applications and robust web services using ASP.NET Core. To start, we'll take a look at the shift from command-line logic to HTTP request and response cycles. We'll understand how controllers, routes, and middleware shape the flow of modern web applications. Next, we'll dive into creating and running a basic ASP.NET Core web API, so we can test and play around with real HTTP endpoints right from our own machines.

The best way to understand how every request flows through the application pipeline is to add and experiment with custom middleware. That way, you'll learn how to intercept or modify requests and responses along the way. We'll also learn to register our own services with the framework's dependency injection container and see the benefits of modular, testable code in action. At last, this chapter is going to teach us to work with configuration files and environment-specific settings. It'll show us to adapt Trackr to different stages of deployment and confirm the settings at runtime.

HTTP Requests and Responses

When we start building web apps with ASP.NET Core, we enter a world that's both familiar and new. The skills we've developed with our console Trackr app, like structuring logic, handling input, and maintaining data, are the foundation of our work. ASP.NET Core builds on these strengths and opens a much wider range of possibilities, allowing our apps to serve many users at once, communicate across the internet, and connect with any client, from browsers to mobile apps and beyond. It's important to understand this shift, so first let's go over some key points.

What Is ASP.NET Core?

The ASP.NET Core is Microsoft's modern, open-source framework for building web applications and APIs. Unlike the classic ASP.NET or desktop tools, ASP.NET Core is cross-platform, cloud-friendly, and designed to run anywhere, from Windows to Linux to containers. It empowers us to create robust web APIs, serve web pages, and handle everything from simple sites to high-performance enterprise backends.

At its heart, the ASP.NET Core brings together several essential building blocks:

- ***Controllers*** that handle incoming HTTP requests, much like how our console app's menu handled user choices
- ***Routing*** that directs each request to the right logic
- ***Middleware*** that processes requests globally, adding cross-cutting features like authentication or logging
- ***Dependency Injection*** that wires our service classes together for testable, modular code

The philosophy is to keep business logic organized in service classes (just like our TaskService), and allow the ASP.NET Core to handle the mechanics of web communication.

We must also understand how the console apps differ from the web apps. And for this, let me quickly draw a direct comparison to ground ourselves:

- ***Console App*** waits for a user command, runs logic, prints a response, and then loops.
- ***ASP.NET Core Web App:*** waits for an HTTP request (from a browser or other client), runs logic, sends back an HTTP response, and immediately becomes ready for the next request.

Instead of a menu-driven loop, the web app responds to independent, stateless requests from many users. Every interaction is a request/response cycle.

Understanding HTTP Request-Response Cycle

Whenever someone interacts with our ASP.NET Core app, by clicking a button, filling a form, or sending data, the client (such as a browser or mobile app) sends an HTTP request to our server. The server processes this request, executes our domain logic, and sends back an HTTP response. This is the fundamental loop of the modern web.

For example:

- The client sends a **`POST /tasks`** request to add a new task, with the task data in JSON.
- ASP.NET Core receives the request, matches it to the correct controller and method using ***routing***.
- The controller invokes our service class (**`TaskService`**), which handles business logic just as it did in the console app.

The result is sent back as an HTTP response, often as JSON data.

Controllers and Routing

In ASP.NET Core, the ***controllers*** take the place of our old console menu and main loop. A controller is a C# class with methods called "actions", each action handles one kind of HTTP request.

For instance, the following is a sample **`TasksController`**:

```
[ApiController]
[Route("[controller]")]
public class TasksController : ControllerBase
{
    [HttpGet]
```

```
    public IActionResult GetAll()
    {
        var tasks = _taskService.GetAll();
        return Ok(tasks);
    }
    [HttpPost]
    public IActionResult Create(TaskItemDto newTask)
    {
        var createdTask = _taskService.Add(newTask);
        return CreatedAtAction(nameof(GetAll), new { id =
createdTask.Id }, createdTask);
    }
}
```

In the above code,

- The **`[Route]`** and **`[HttpGet]`** / **`[HttpPost]`** attributes define how URLs map to methods.
- Routing is automatic: a **`GET /tasks`** request triggers **`GetAll`**, a **`POST /tasks`** triggers **`Create`**. And,
- Controllers call our domain logic in **`TaskService`**, keeping responsibilities cleanly separated.

Middleware Overvieew

Middleware is basically a set of tools that sits between the HTTP request and our controllers. Think about having global features in the console app, like logging every command or checking authentication, but applied to every web request automatically.

In ASP.NET Core, there are a few ways middleware can help. They can:

- Keep track of requests and responses.
- Handle errors and format responses.
- Make sure you're following the security rules.
- You can change the data or headers.

We can add such middleware to the application pipeline, and every request goes through it before and after reaching the controllers.

The existing **TaskService** logic is still the engine of Trackr, but now it is used by the controllers instead of by a console loop. For example, when a client sends a request to create a task, the controller receives the data and calls **TaskService.Add**, just as before, but instead of writing to the terminal, it returns an HTTP response.

Following is a quick look at the Console vs. Web:

Console App	ASP.NET Core Web App
Console menu handles input	Controller receives HTTP request
User chooses option, enters data	Client sends data as JSON
Service class processes logic	Controller calls service class
Console.WriteLine outputs response	Controller returns HTTP response
Single user, one loop	Many users, many requests

Creating Task via HTTP

To quickly create a task via http, we can do it in the following request:

- The client sends a POST request to **/tasks** with task data.
- ASP.NET Core's routing sends the request to **TasksController.Create**.
- The controller validates the input, calls **TaskService.Add**, and creates the task.
- The result is returned as a JSON HTTP response with status 201 (Created).

Here, no more **Console.ReadLine()** or **Console.WriteLine()**. Rather, our app now speaks HTTP, and the logic we wrote before is just as useful.

Every menu option we wrote in the console becomes a web endpoint, every output becomes a response, and the robust, testable logic in our service classes continues to power the application behind the scenes.

Building Minimal ASP.NET Core App

We have come far with our Trackr project in the console world. Now, imagine that our goal is to make Trackr's features available to anyone, on any browser, from any device, or even to a mobile app. To make that happen, we need to turn Trackr into a web service. This is where ASP.NET Core comes in.

Building our first ASP.NET Core app might feel like uncharted territory, but when we start small and relate each step to what we already know, it becomes a natural next move. Let us do this together, so by the end of this topic, we can bring up a working web API, test it with a real HTTP request, and understand how it all fits together.

Creating Web Service

We will set up a new project just for our Trackr web API:

```
dotnet new webapi -n TrackrWebApi --no-https
cd TrackrWebApi
```

The Visual Studio Code can open this folder, giving us a familiar workspace. And, you can notice a few things like a **Program.cs**, a **Controllers** folder, and some sample files.

Program Structure

We then now open the **Program.cs**. Compared to our old **Main** method in the console app, this file is where the web server is wired up and the API endpoints are made available.

The following is the essence of what .NET 9 gives us by default:

```
var builder = WebApplication.CreateBuilder(args);
builder.Services.AddControllers();
var app = builder.Build();
app.MapControllers();
app.Run();
```

The above one includes:

- ***CreateBuilder*** sets up the foundation (like initializing services, configuration, and logging).
- ***AddControllers*** prepares the app to recognize controllers, these will soon hold Trackr's endpoints.
- ***Build and MapControllers*** bundles everything and activates routing, so HTTP requests know which controller to reach. And,
- ***Run*** boots up the server and listens for incoming requests, just as our console app waited for user input.

Adding Simple Endpoint

Next, inside the **Controllers** folder, we will now make a new file named

TasksController.cs. Here, we want to bring Trackr to life with a simple HTTP response:

```
using Microsoft.AspNetCore.Mvc;
[ApiController]
[Route("[controller]")]
public class TasksController : ControllerBase
{
    [HttpGet]
    public IActionResult Get()
    {
        return Ok(new { message = "Trackr is running as a web service!" });
    }
}
```

Now, what we have here is the web version of our Trackr's console greeting. Anyone who asks for **/tasks** will get a friendly message in return.

Running Web Service

Back in the terminal, we will then start the app:

```
dotnet run
```

We will look at the output and see:

```
Now listening on: http://localhost:5000
```

Now for the real test, we go to **http://localhost:5000/tasks** and can see a JSON response:

```
{
    "message": "Trackr is running as a web service!"
}
```

This is the "Hello World" moment for our web API. We can also use a REST client like Postman or Insomnia to send the same GET request.

Inspecting Program.cs Pipeline

In the above, I will show you the break down on why our HTTP request gets a response:

- The app runs and listens for requests.
- The **[ApiController]** and **[Route]** attributes tell ASP.NET Core to match **GET /tasks** with our **Get** method.
- **AddControllers** ensures that all **[Controller]** classes are recognized.
- **MapControllers** connects the routing engine to our controller logic.

So here, nothing is hidden or magical. Each step is visible in **Program.cs**, from setup, to controller registration, to running the app. Unlike the console app, where everything happened in a loop, the web app is always listening and ready to serve requests to anyone who asks.

Sample Program

For now, take a look at our setup. If you edit the greeting message, restart the app, and check the browser, you'll see the change right away. Or, add a new method for a different HTTP verb. It's really straightforward. Everything responds right away, no menu, no loop, just clean, direct endpoints.

If we want to add a POST endpoint, it would look like this:

```
[HttpPost]
public IActionResult Create([FromBody] TaskItemDto newTask)
{
    // For now, just echo back what was sent
    return Ok(new { received = newTask });
}
```

We can try it using a REST client by sending a POST request with a sample JSON body.

By taking these small steps, we did not just “see a web API”, we built, ran, and verified it for ourselves. Now, the line between console logic and HTTP endpoints feels tangible. We can bootstrap a new web service, confirm it works, and start layering in the logic we know.

The next time we want to expose any functionality, we just have to add a new controller or action, restart, and see the update. This is the heart of rapid, confident web development in ASP.NET Core.

HTTP Request Pipeline and Middleware

Given that Trackr is now responding to HTTP requests, let's take a look at how each request makes its way through our ASP.NET Core application. It's like every HTTP request is a traveler passing through a series of gates. And each gate is a piece of middleware. These gates can inspect, modify, log, or even short-circuit the request. But if we add our own gate (custom middleware), we'll see exactly where our logic fits and how requests flow, get transformed, and eventually reach our controllers. If we work together on this, we can make the invisible journey of every HTTP request visible and intuitive.

Adding Custom Middleware

We will start by writing a custom middleware that logs every HTTP request Trackr receives. So here, we will add a file called **RequestLoggingMiddleware.cs** to our project:

```
public class RequestLoggingMiddleware
{
    private readonly RequestDelegate _next;
    public RequestLoggingMiddleware(RequestDelegate next)
    {
        _next = next;
    }
    public async Task InvokeAsync(HttpContext context)
    {
        Console.WriteLine($"[{DateTime.Now:T}]
{context.Request.Method} {context.Request.Path} received.");
        await _next(context); // Let the request continue
through the pipeline
    }
}
```

This middleware prints every request's method and path with a timestamp. By calling **_next(context)**, it allows the request to move to the next gate.

Now, in **Program.cs**, before our controllers are mapped, we will then add:

```
app.UseMiddleware<RequestLoggingMiddleware>();
```

We will place this line just after building the app, but before **`app.MapControllers()`**. This ensures every request is logged, right at the start of its journey.

Observing Real-Time Flow

We will now run our app and send a few requests to **`/tasks`** using a browser or REST client. After watching the console, each request immediately logs a line like:

```
[12:04:15] GET /tasks received.
```

If we send multiple requests quickly, we will see each one logged, even before any controller action is reached. This proves our middleware is acting as the first checkpoint for every request coming in.

Returning Response

Next, we will experiment further. Suppose we want to create a maintenance window, when anyone requests **`/diagnostics`**, we want to respond with a simple message and not let the request continue.

So here, we will update our middleware:

```
public async Task InvokeAsync(HttpContext context)
{
    if
(context.Request.Path.StartsWithSegments("/diagnostics"))
    {
        Console.WriteLine("Diagnostics endpoint hit. Sending
health check response.");
        context.Response.ContentType = "text/plain";
        await context.Response.WriteAsync("Diagnostics check:
pipeline is healthy.");
        return; // The request will stop here, no further
middleware or controller will run
    }
    Console.WriteLine($"[{DateTime.Now:T}]
{context.Request.Method} {context.Request.Path} received.");
    await _next(context); // Pass to the next middleware or
controller
```

```
}
```

If we visit **/diagnostics**, we will immediately see the health message in the browser, and notice our controller for **/diagnostics** (if any) will never run. For all other requests, the normal pipeline continues.

Order and Interaction

If we want to add another middleware that marks when a request has finished processing. For this, in **Program.cs**, after our first middleware, we then must add:

```
app.Use(async (context, next) =>
{
    Console.WriteLine("Second middleware before controller.");
    await next();
    Console.WriteLine("Second middleware after controller.");
});
```

Now, when we send a request, we must keep watching together what appears in our console:

```
[12:09:03] GET /tasks received.
Second middleware before controller.
Second middleware after controller.
```

So here, we see that the request flows through each middleware in the order we have registered them. Our custom logger runs first, then the second middleware says "before controller." Once the controller sends a response, the pipeline starts unwinding, and the message "after controller" prints, this is true post-processing, happening on the way back out.

If our pipeline had five middlewares, we would see the request step in through each one, then step out in the reverse order. This helps us predict exactly where to put logging, error handling, or security checks.

Built-in Middleware

The ASP.NET Core has several built-in middleware, such as **UseRouting**, **UseAuthorization**, and others. Their order also shapes the journey.

For example:

- If we add our custom logger before **UseRouting**, it will log every request, regardless of whether it matches a controller or not.

- If we add authentication middleware, it will block unauthorized requests before our controller logic ever runs.

So here, we can try moving our middleware around and see what happens. If we move our logger after **app.MapControllers()**, we will notice it never runs for controller requests, proving how order changes behavior.

For example, let us try what if we wanted to reject all requests made after 6 PM? For this, in our logger middleware, we could add:

```
if (DateTime.Now.Hour >= 18)

{

    context.Response.StatusCode = 403;

    await context.Response.WriteAsync("Trackr is unavailable after 6 PM.");

    return;

}
```

Now, we try sending a request after 6 PM, and instantly see our custom response, with the request stopped in its tracks, no controller ever gets called.

With this, we understand exactly how every HTTP request step through our application, who gets to inspect it, when it can be stopped or modified, and how the flow is orchestrated. This awareness prepares us to add sophisticated features, like security, error handling, or analytics, confidently and predictably.

Registering Services with DI Container

Now that we have built up Trackr as a web service, we are ready to make our application truly modular and testable. This is where ASP.NET Core's built-in ***Dependency Injection (DI) container*** comes into play. Rather than having our controllers directly create or manage instances of **TaskService**, we want the framework to provide these dependencies automatically. This makes our code more flexible, easier to maintain, and much simpler to test.

In our console app, we called **TaskService** methods directly or used static classes. In a growing web app, this pattern can quickly lead to tight coupling, making it hard to swap implementations, add logging, or write unit tests. The DI flips the script, where instead of each controller constructing its own services, the ASP.NET Core creates and supplies these dependencies as needed. This makes the application architecture cleaner and more maintainable.

Refactoring TaskService

First, we will refactor **TaskService** so it can be used as an instance (not just static methods). For this, in **TaskService.cs**, we will rewrite the class:

```
public class TaskService : ITaskService
{
    private readonly List<TaskItem> _tasks = new();
    private int _nextId = 1;
    public IEnumerable<TaskItem> GetAll()
    {
        return _tasks;
    }
    public TaskItem Add(TaskItemDto dto)
    {
        var newTask = new TaskItem(_nextId++, dto.Title,
dto.DueDate);
        _tasks.Add(newTask);
        return newTask;
    }
    public bool Complete(int id)
    {
        var task = _tasks.FirstOrDefault(t => t.Id == id);
        if (task == null) return false;
        task.IsCompleted = true;
        return true;
    }
}
```

Next, we will then define an interface for best practice:

```
public interface ITaskService
{
    IEnumerable<TaskItem> GetAll();
```

```
    TaskItem Add(TaskItemDto dto);
    bool Complete(int id);
}
```

Registering TaskService in DI Container

We will now plug **TaskService** into ASP.NET Core's DI system. And, we do this in **Program.cs**, where the services are configured:

```
var builder = WebApplication.CreateBuilder(args);
// Register TaskService as a service with scoped lifetime
builder.Services.AddScoped<ITaskService, TaskService>();
builder.Services.AddControllers();
var app = builder.Build();
app.UseMiddleware<RequestLoggingMiddleware>();
app.MapControllers();
app.Run();
```

Here, in the above:

- **AddScoped** means one instance of **TaskService** will be created per HTTP request.
- We reference the service by its interface (**ITaskService**) so it can be easily swapped in tests or future refactoring.

Injecting TaskService into Controllers

After this, our controllers can receive **TaskService** as a constructor parameter, and the ASP.NET Core will supply it automatically.

Hence, we will now update **TasksController**:

```
[ApiController]
[Route("[controller]")]
public class TasksController : ControllerBase
{
    private readonly ITaskService _taskService;
```

```
    public TasksController(ITaskService taskService)
    {
        _taskService = taskService;
    }
    [HttpGet]
    public IActionResult GetAll()
    {
        var tasks = _taskService.GetAll();
        return Ok(tasks);
    }
    [HttpPost]
    public IActionResult Create(TaskItemDto dto)
    {
        var created = _taskService.Add(dto);
        return CreatedAtAction(nameof(GetAll), new { id =
created.Id }, created);
    }
    [HttpPatch("{id}/complete")]
    public IActionResult Complete(int id)
    {
        var success = _taskService.Complete(id);
        if (!success) return NotFound();
        return NoContent();
    }
}
```

We are not required to create or manage **TaskService** instances directly. The ASP.NET Core's DI system ensures each controller action receives a fresh, ready-to-use service.

Running and Testing Integration

Since everything is done, we will now run the web service with **dotnet run**, then send some requests:

- Use **GET /tasks** to retrieve all tasks.
- Use **POST /tasks** with JSON data to create a new task.
- Use **PATCH /tasks/{id}/complete** to mark a task as completed.

After this, each action will work as expected. The service is injected, tracked, and managed for us. If we ever want to swap out **TaskService** for a mock or an upgraded version, we only need to change the DI registration, no controller code needs to change.

Configuration and Environments

Almost all the applications run in development, staging, and production, and each run with their own settings for things like connection strings, feature flags, or external service URLs. The ASP.NET Core gives us robust, built-in tools for handling configuration and environment-specific values. So here in this topic, we will explore to read configuration from **appsettings.json**, override values per environment, and check the current environment at runtime.

Reading Configuration

By default, every new ASP.NET Core project includes an **appsettings.json** file. This file is the central place for storing configuration, such as connection strings, application settings, and feature toggles, in a structured JSON format.

Here, we will first open **appsettings.json** and we will see something like:

```
{
  "Logging": {
    "LogLevel": {
      "Default": "Information",
      "Microsoft": "Warning"
    }
  },
  "AllowedHosts": "*",
  "TrackrSettings": {
    "WelcomeMessage": "Welcome to Trackr Web API!"
  }
```

```
}
```

Now here, suppose we want to read the custom **WelcomeMessage** from this file and display it from our controller. For this, we will inject the configuration provider into our controller:

```
using Microsoft.Extensions.Configuration;
[ApiController]
[Route("[controller]")]
public class HomeController : ControllerBase
{
    private readonly IConfiguration _config;
    public HomeController(IConfiguration config)
    {
        _config = config;
    }
    [HttpGet]
    public IActionResult GetWelcome()
    {
        string message =
_config["TrackrSettings:WelcomeMessage"];
        return Ok(new { message });
    }
}
```

Now, when we hit **/home**, the controller reads the welcome message directly from **appsettings.json**.

Overriding Configuration per Environment

Often, we want different values for different environments. For instance, we may want a "Testing mode enabled" message in development, and a friendlier message in production.

The ASP.NET Core automatically loads **appsettings.{Environment}.json** (such as **appsettings.Development.json** or **appsettings.Production.json**) based on the current environment.

Add Environment-Specific Settings file

We will create an **appsettings.Development.json** file with this content:

```
{
  "TrackrSettings": {
    "WelcomeMessage": "Welcome to Trackr (Development)!"
  }
}
```

When our app runs in Development mode, this value will override the one in **appsettings.json**.

Run in Specific Environment

By default, running with **dotnet run** sets the environment to Development on local machines. However, we can also explicitly set the environment variable:

```
$env:ASPNETCORE_ENVIRONMENT="Production"
dotnet run
```

Now, depending on the environment, the ASP.NET Core merges settings from both **appsettings.json** and the environment-specific file, using the most specific value available.

Checking Current Environment at Runtime

Sometimes, we want to write code that behaves differently depending on the environment. ASP.NET Core provides an **IWebHostEnvironment** service for this.

So here, we will update our controller:

```
using Microsoft.AspNetCore.Hosting;
[ApiController]
[Route("[controller]")]
public class HomeController : ControllerBase
{
    private readonly IConfiguration _config;
    private readonly IWebHostEnvironment _env;
```

```
    public HomeController(IConfiguration config,
IWebHostEnvironment env)
    {
        _config = config;
        _env = env;
    }
    [HttpGet]
    public IActionResult GetWelcome()
    {
        string message =
_config["TrackrSettings:WelcomeMessage"];
        string envName = _env.EnvironmentName;
        return Ok(new { message, environment = envName });
    }
}
```

When we access **/home**, the response now includes both the welcome message and the current environment name, so we can always verify where our app is running.

With this setup, we can:

- Safely store and read configuration data for any setting, at any level of complexity.
- Adapt our app to different environments, using local databases for development, test settings for QA, and production databases and services for release.
- Display or log values to confirm our app is running in the correct environment, preventing configuration mistakes and misdeployments.

Summary

Throughout this chapter, we moved from our console-based Trackr app to a modern ASP.NET Core web application, learning how each part of the framework fits into a real-world development workflow. We created and launched a basic web API, watched Trackr respond to real HTTP requests, and confirmed our endpoints were working from both browsers and REST clients. We built and inserted custom middleware to see in real time how every request went through the pipeline.

We then registered our TaskService with the built-in DI container and injected it into controllers, making Trackr's logic modular and testable. At last, we took a look at how to handle application configuration using **appsettings.json**, override settings for different environments, and programmatically check the runtime environment. These experiences helped us build the confidence to bootstrap, configure, and operate robust web services using ASP.NET Core.

CHAPTER 6: ROUTING AND WEB API CONTROLLERS

Overview

In this chapter, we're going to take a look at how ASP.NET Core handles routing and Web API controllers to deliver a predictable, maintainable, and professional API. To start, we'll set up endpoint routing, which'll show us exactly how controllers are registered and mapped to URLs when they're running. We'll get hands-on practice designing and testing attribute-based routes, using parameters and patterns to control which URLs trigger which actions.

With the **`[ApiController]`** attribute, we can take advantage of automatic model binding and validation. We'll show you how to bind models from route segments, query strings, and request bodies, giving you a complete toolkit for accepting input in every common web scenario. This chapter will also show us how to use disciplined HTTP status codes and problem details, making sure that every API response is meaningful and standards-based.

Configuring Endpoint Routing

Now that we are aiming to further develop Trackr into a fully-featured web API, we shall explore more on how incoming HTTP requests are routed to our code. The ASP.NET Core uses endpoint routing to match URLs to controllers and their actions. The place where we configure this is in our **`Program.cs`**, and by implementing the basics very well, we can get to know exactly how our application exposes its features as HTTP endpoints.

In the following, we will know how to configure endpoint routing, confirm our controllers are being discovered, and see exactly which URLs are mapped to our code at runtime.

Wiring up MapControllers

To start with, we will open **`Program.cs`** in our Trackr project. Here, the most important line for endpoint routing is:

```
app.MapControllers();
```

This command tells ASP.NET Core: "Look for all controller classes in the project and create routes based on their attributes and conventions." We always place this after adding controllers and configuring any middleware.

Now here, a typical setup generally looks like this:

```
var builder = WebApplication.CreateBuilder(args);
builder.Services.AddControllers();
var app = builder.Build();
app.UseMiddleware<RequestLoggingMiddleware>();
```

```
app.MapControllers();
app.Run();
```

With this configuration, any controller with **[ApiController]** and **[Route]** attributes will be automatically registered as an endpoint.

Testing Controller Discovery and Endpoint Mapping

We will now verify that Trackr's controllers are being picked up correctly. For this, we will make sure that we have a controller, such as **TasksController**:

```
[ApiController]
[Route("[controller]")]
public class TasksController : ControllerBase
{
    [HttpGet]
    public IActionResult Get() => Ok(new { status = "Trackr
running!" });
}
```

After this, we then run the application using **dotnet run**. The console output will include startup information, but not the actual routes by default.

Now, to test endpoint discovery, we visit **http://localhost:5000/tasks**. If we get a response (for example, **{ "status": "Trackr running!" }**), we have confirmed our controller is mapped and reachable. If there is a 404 error, we check the route attribute or controller naming.

Viewing Active Routes at Runtime

Sometimes, we may want to see all registered endpoints in one place, especially useful as the application grows. The ASP.NET Core allows us to expose this information with a little help from a built-in diagnostic package.

Add Endpoint Routing Diagnostics Middleware

In **Program.cs**, we will add the following line before **app.MapControllers();**:

```
app.UseEndpoints(endpoints =>
{
```

```
    endpoints.MapControllers();
    endpoints.MapGet("/endpoints", async context =>
    {
        var dataSource =
app.Services.GetRequiredService<EndpointDataSource>();
        var sb = new System.Text.StringBuilder();
        foreach (var endpoint in dataSource.Endpoints)
        {
            sb.AppendLine(endpoint.DisplayName);
        }
        await context.Response.WriteAsync(sb.ToString());
    });
});
```

For minimal APIs in .NET 9, we can directly inject the **EndpointDataSource**:

```
app.MapGet("/endpoints", (EndpointDataSource
endpointDataSource) =>
    string.Join('\n', endpointDataSource.Endpoints.Select(e =>
e.DisplayName)));
```

Check Active Endpoints

Now, after starting the application, we will visit **http://localhost:5000/endpoints**. Here, we will see a list of all routes that are currently active in the app, such as:

```
TasksController.Get (GET)
```

or

```
GET /tasks
```

This shows, in real time, which controllers and actions are exposed, making it easy for us to verify that our code is mapped as we intend.

One must understand here that how these URLs are matched to code. So here, when a request arrives (for example, **GET /tasks**), the ASP.NET Core:

- Reads the HTTP method (GET, POST, etc.) and path (**/tasks**)
- Compares it to all registered routes from controller attributes
- Finds the best match and invokes the corresponding controller action

If the path does not match any registered route, the framework returns a 404 Not Found.

By controlling the **[Route]** and **[HttpGet]**, **[HttpPost]**, etc., attributes in our controllers, we can define exactly which URLs are mapped to which code, giving us precise control over our API's shape.

This skill becomes essential as our API grows and as others begin to consume our endpoints.

Attribute Routing on Controllers and Actions

When building a flexible and user-friendly API, it's crucial to have total control over how our URLs are mapped to code. Attribute routing gives us a lot of control over this process because we can define routes directly on controllers and their actions. In this topic, we're going to create a **TasksController** for Trackr, apply various route attributes, including parameters, and then test different URL patterns to see how ASP.NET Core matches incoming requests to our code.

Creating TasksController

So here, we will first start by defining a basic controller for our tasks. In the **Controllers** folder, we will create a file called **TasksController.cs**:

```
using Microsoft.AspNetCore.Mvc;
[ApiController]
[Route("api/tasks")]
public class TasksController : ControllerBase
{
    [HttpGet]
    public IActionResult GetAll()
    {
        // Simulate fetching all tasks
        return Ok(new[] {
            new { Id = 1, Title = "First Task" },
            new { Id = 2, Title = "Second Task" }
```

```
        });
    }
}
```

Here, we have set a ***route prefix*** of **"api/tasks"** on the controller. Every action inside this controller will now be reachable with URLs starting with **/api/tasks**.

Adding Route Attributes with Parameters

Next, we will now expand our controller by adding actions with route parameters. These allow us to handle URLs like **/api/tasks/3** for retrieving a specific task by its ID.

```
[ApiController]
[Route("api/tasks")]
public class TasksController : ControllerBase
{
    [HttpGet]
    public IActionResult GetAll()
    {
        // Return all tasks
        return Ok(new[] {
            new { Id = 1, Title = "First Task" },
            new { Id = 2, Title = "Second Task" }
        });
    }
    [HttpGet("{id}")]
    public IActionResult GetById(int id)
    {
        // Simulate fetching a single task
        var task = new { Id = id, Title = $"Task {id}" };
        return Ok(task);
    }
    [HttpPost]
```

```
    public IActionResult Create([FromBody] object newTask)
    {
        // Simulate creating a new task
        return CreatedAtAction(nameof(GetById), new { id = 3
}, newTask);
    }
}
```

In the above,

- The **[HttpGet("{id}")]** attribute creates a route for **/api/tasks/3**, mapping the **id** segment of the URL directly to the method's **id** parameter. And,
- The **[HttpPost]** attribute means **POST /api/tasks** will trigger the **Create** action.

We can furhter expand this to add custom routes for other actions as needed, such as marking a task as complete:

```
[HttpPatch("{id}/complete")]
public IActionResult Complete(int id)
{
    // Simulate completing a task
    return NoContent();
}
```

This will match requests to **/api/tasks/3/complete**.

Testing URL Patterns and Routing

After this, we will now verify that our attribute routing works as intended. For this, we will start the app, then try these endpoints with a browser or REST client:

```
GET http://localhost:5000/api/tasks
```

This returns the list of all tasks.

```
GET http://localhost:5000/api/tasks/2
```

And this one returns a single task with Id 2.

```
POST http://localhost:5000/api/tasks
```

This one simulates creating a new task.

```
PATCH http://localhost:5000/api/tasks/1/complete
```

This one marks the task 1 as complete.

If we send requests that do not match any route, for example, **GET /api/tasks/abc** where **abc** is not an integer, the ASP.NET Core will return a 404 Not Found.

You can try adding the own actions with custom routes, such as:

```
[HttpGet("search/{keyword}")]
public IActionResult Search(string keyword)
{
    // Simulate searching for tasks by keyword
    return Ok(new[] { new { Id = 10, Title = $"Task matching
'{keyword}'" } });
}
```

Here, the **GET /api/tasks/search/urgent** will return any tasks with "urgent" in the title.

With this, we can handle any URL structure our application needs, test them quickly, and ensure every endpoint in Trackr is discoverable, predictable, and easy for clients to use.

Designing Web API Controllers with [ApiController]

If we want to develop solid and user-friendly Web APIs in ASP.NET Core, we should make the most of features that make our controllers concise, reliable, and secure. One of the best tools for this is the **[ApiController]** attribute. By putting **[ApiController]** in our controllers, we get automatic model validation, better binding behavior, and built-in error responses. This frees us from writing repetitive manual checks and boilerplate code.

So, we should just take it step by step and see exactly how **[ApiController]** changes our workflow and makes our APIs clearer and safer.

Annotating Controller with [ApiController]

To start with, we will first look at the difference **[ApiController]** makes.

Then, in our **TasksController**, we will then add the attribute just above the class declaration:

```
using Microsoft.AspNetCore.Mvc;
[ApiController]
[Route("api/tasks")]
public class TasksController : ControllerBase
{
    // Actions will go here
}
```

With this single line, the ASP.NET Core treats this class as a special kind of controller designed for APIs, enabling several enhancements out of the box.

Automatic Model Binding and Validation

One of the key benefits of **[ApiController]** is ***automatic model binding and validation***. This means whenever a client sends JSON or other data in a request, the ASP.NET Core will automatically:

- Attempt to bind it to our action's parameter (such as a DTO class)
- Validate it according to data annotations on our model (such as **[Required]**, **[StringLength]**, etc). And,
- Return a detailed **400 Bad Request** error if validation fails, before our code runs

In the following, we will define a DTO with validation attributes:

```
public class TaskCreateDto
{
    [Required]
    [StringLength(100)]
    public string Title { get; set; }
    public DateTime? DueDate { get; set; }
}
```

Next, in our controller, we will then write an action:

```
[HttpPost]
public IActionResult Create([FromBody] TaskCreateDto dto)
{
    // If the model is invalid, this code will never be
reached
    var createdTask = new { Id = 101, dto.Title, dto.DueDate
};
    return CreatedAtAction(nameof(GetById), new { id = 101 },
createdTask);
}
```

With **`[ApiController]`**, if a client sends a request with an empty or missing **`Title`**, ASP.NET Core automatically detects the problem and returns a response like:

```
{
    "errors": {
        "Title": ["The Title field is required."]
    },
    "type": "https://tools.ietf.org/html/rfc7231#section-
6.5.1",
    "title": "One or more validation errors occurred.",
    "status": 400,
    "traceId": "|..."
}
```

Here, there is no need for manual **`if (!ModelState.IsValid)`** checks or crafting error responses by hand. It keeps our controller actions focused on business logic only.

Convenient and Safe Model Binding

With **`[ApiController]`**, the model binding is more reliable and predictable:

- If the request body is missing or malformed, the framework rejects the request with a clear **`400 Bad Request`**.
- Route parameters and query strings are also automatically validated and bound to action parameters.

For example, if we define:

```
[HttpGet("{id}")]
public IActionResult GetById(int id)
{
    // id is always present and bound from the URL
    var task = new { Id = id, Title = $"Task {id}" };
    return Ok(task);
}
```

If the client sends **`GET /api/tasks/abc`**, the framework returns a **`400 Bad Request`** automatically, since **`abc`** cannot be bound to an integer.

You can try sending requests with invalid or incomplete data using Postman or a REST client. And, then just watch how the API returns detailed, helpful error messages without any extra code in our controller. If we fix the request, the action succeeds as expected.

By embracing **`[ApiController]`**, we are not just following best practices, we are leveraging the full power of ASP.NET Core to deliver safe, reliable, and idiomatic Web APIs, all while writing less code and spending more time on our application's business logic.

Model Binding from Route, Query, and Body

A Web API's strength comes from accepting input in flexible, safe ways, whether that input arrives as a URL segment, a query string, or JSON in the request body. So here, we will work together to see how ASP.NET Core automatically binds incoming data from each of these sources to our action method parameters and request models. We will also practice validating this input and returning clear, meaningful error responses if the data does not meet our expectations.

Binding from Route Segments

To start, we will begin with route segments. They are portions of the URL path captured as variables. Suppose we want to fetch a specific task by its unique Id. So here, in our controller, we will define the following:

```
[HttpGet("{id}")]
public IActionResult GetById(int id)
{
    // id is bound from the URL, for example: /api/tasks/42
```

```
    if (id <= 0)
        return BadRequest(new { error = "Id must be positive."
});
    var task = new { Id = id, Title = $"Task {id}" };
    return Ok(task);
}
```

In the above, **{id}** in the route tells ASP.NET Core to extract that value from the URL and pass it as the **id** parameter. If the client requests **/api/tasks/5**, **id** will be **5**. If they send **/api/tasks/-2**, our validation will catch it and return a helpful error.

Binding from Query Strings

The query strings are key-value pairs appended to the URL after a question mark, such as **/api/tasks/search?keyword=urgent**. These are often used for filtering, sorting, or paging.

In the following, we will add a search action:

```
[HttpGet("search")]
public IActionResult Search([FromQuery] string keyword)
{
    if (string.IsNullOrWhiteSpace(keyword))
        return BadRequest(new { error = "Keyword is required."
});
    // Simulate search results
    var results = new[] { new { Id = 1, Title = $"Urgent Task:
{keyword}" } };
    return Ok(results);
}
```

With the **[FromQuery]**, the ASP.NET Core looks for **keyword** in the query string. If the client forgets to provide a value, we return a clear error. Otherwise, the logic proceeds as intended.

Binding from Body (JSON)

The most common pattern for POST or PUT requests is to accept a structured object as JSON in the body.

In the above, we will define a DTO:

```
public class TaskCreateDto
{
    [Required]
    [StringLength(100)]
    public string Title { get; set; }
    public DateTime? DueDate { get; set; }
}
```

Then, our controller action:

```
[HttpPost]
public IActionResult Create([FromBody] TaskCreateDto dto)
{
    // With [ApiController], ASP.NET Core auto-validates dto
    if (!ModelState.IsValid)
        return ValidationProblem(ModelState);
    // Create the task
    var created = new { Id = 999, dto.Title, dto.DueDate };
    return CreatedAtAction(nameof(GetById), new { id = 999 },
created);
}
```

Since we are using **`[ApiController]`**, the ASP.NET Core will automatically reject requests with missing or invalid data (such as empty **`Title`**) and return a detailed **`400 Bad Request`** with all validation errors.

Combining Binding Sources

Sometimes, an action needs to bind from several sources at once:

```
[HttpPut("{id}")]
public IActionResult Update(int id, [FromBody] TaskCreateDto
dto, [FromQuery] bool markComplete = false)
```

```
{
    if (!ModelState.IsValid)
        return ValidationProblem(ModelState);
    // Simulate update
    var updated = new { Id = id, dto.Title, dto.DueDate,
IsCompleted = markComplete };
    return Ok(updated);
}
```

Here, the **`id`** comes from the route, the request body provides the main update data, and **`markComplete`** can be toggled with a query string (**`?markComplete=true`**). The ASP.NET Core brings all these together into our parameters, ready to use, and already validated.

Using all such patterns, we can easily aim to become fluent in accepting input safely and predictably in every corner of Trackr, and any future ASP.NET Core API we build.

Returning Results, Status Codes, and Problem Details

There's more to writing a disciplined Web API than just getting the logic right. The right HTTP status codes and structured results are also key. When our Trackr controllers send back clear signals, like 201 Created after creating a task, 204 No Content after a successful update, 404 Not Found for missing resources, or detailed validation errors, clients and users always know exactly what happened. This predictability is key to creating solid and easy-to-maintain web APIs.

We'll build this skill together, step by step, using real actions and responses that'll make our API easy to integrate, debug, and trust.

Returning Success

200 OK

For actions that fetch or update resources and return data, we use **`Ok()`**:

```
[HttpGet("{id}")]
public IActionResult GetById(int id)
{
    var task = TaskStore.Get(id);
```

```
    if (task == null)
        return NotFound(); // 404
    return Ok(task); // 200
}
```

201 Created

After creating a new resource, we return 201 and include a Location header pointing to the new resource. The ASP.NET Core provides **`CreatedAtAction`**:

```
[HttpPost]
public IActionResult Create([FromBody] TaskCreateDto dto)
{
    var createdTask = TaskStore.Add(dto);
    return CreatedAtAction(nameof(GetById), new { id =
createdTask.Id }, createdTask);
}
```

This tells clients both where to find the resource and what data was created.

204 No Content

For actions like marking a task as complete or deleting a resource, when there is nothing more to return, we will use **`NoContent()`**:

```
[HttpPatch("{id}/complete")]
public IActionResult Complete(int id)
{
    var success = TaskStore.MarkComplete(id);
    if (!success)
        return NotFound();
    return NoContent(); // 204
}
```

Returning Not Found (404)

If the client requests a resource that does not exist, **NotFound()** signals this unambiguously:

```
[HttpGet("{id}")]
public IActionResult GetById(int id)
{
    var task = TaskStore.Get(id);
    if (task == null)
        return NotFound(); // 404
    return Ok(task);
}
```

The response is empty or can contain a brief explanation, but the status code does the talking.

Bad Request with Problem Details (400)

When input fails validation (missing required fields, invalid types), the **[ApiController]** helps us by returning a standardized 400 Bad Request response that includes ***problem details***.

So, if a client sends a **POST** without a **Title**, then they get:

```
{
    "errors": {
        "Title": ["The Title field is required."]
    },
    "type": "https://tools.ietf.org/html/rfc7231#section-
6.5.1",
    "title": "One or more validation errors occurred.",
    "status": 400,
    "traceId": "|..."
}
```

If we want to add our own custom validation in the controller, we can return a problem response explicitly:

```
if (dto.DueDate < DateTime.Today)
    return Problem(
```

```
        detail: "DueDate cannot be in the past.",
        statusCode: 400,
        title: "Invalid Task Data"
    );
```

The ASP.NET Core's **Problem()** helper ensures our errors are clear, machine-readable, and consistent.

Following is the summary table highlighting the common status codes in Web APIs:

Scenario	Method	Status Code	ASP.NET Core Helper
Fetch resource	**GET /api/tasks/5**	200	**Ok(result)**
Resource created	**POST /api/tasks**	201	**CreatedAtAction(...)**
Resource not found	**GET /api/tasks/99**	404	**NotFound()**
Successful update/delete	**PATCH/DELETE /api/tasks/5**	204	**NoContent()**
Validation failure	Invalid input	400	Automatic / **Problem()**

And with our API, you'll get clear responses with HTTP status codes and well-organized results, making it easy to tell if something worked or not. They can build reliable integrations, handle errors gracefully, and users receive instant, helpful feedback. We're using HTTP semantics to make sure our web API always stays solid, predictable, and professional, no matter how complex the requirements get.

Summary

To sum up, we learned how ASP.NET Core matches incoming HTTP requests to our Web API code, building a solid mental model for how routing and controllers work together. We practiced configuring endpoint routing in Program.cs with **MapControllers**, and verified that all our controllers were being discovered and mapped correctly to URLs. We created a **TasksController** and applied attribute routing, adding route parameters and designing URL patterns to match specific actions and data, which allowed us to see firsthand how precise and flexible route matching can be. By annotating our controllers with **[ApiController]**, we benefited from automatic model binding, input validation, and clear error responses, which reduced the need for repetitive manual error checking.

Later, we then worked with model binding from multiple sources, including route segments, query strings, and request bodies, ensuring our APIs could safely and predictably accept input in any format. Finally, we implemented actions that returned disciplined HTTP status codes, such as 201 for creation, 204 for no content, 404 for not found, and 400 for validation errors, always providing structured responses that clients can depend on.

CHAPTER 7: UP AND RUNNING WITH SQL SERVER EXPRESS

Overview

In this chapter, we're going to take it up a notch and start working with a real relational database, SQL Server Express, instead of just playing around in our memory. We'll start by introducing SQL Server Express, then we'll walk through the installation and show you how to connect to our local database using SQL Server Management Studio. We'll practice designing tables that accurately represent tasks, users, and categories for our Trackr app, and learn to define primary keys and set up relationships between entities with foreign keys.

Then, the chapter will teach us to write basic SQL queries for inserting, updating, deleting, and retrieving data, including how to use joins to pull related data together. We'll explore to use transactions to keep multi-step operations safe and atomic, and see firsthand how integrity constraints help us maintain reliable, clean data even when mistakes occur. To get a little more familiar with the skills, we'll build a simple C# console utility that uses ADO.NET to connect to SQL Server Express, sends commands, and processes results. By the time you're done with this chapter, you'll have the hands-on skills and the big-picture knowledge to build, debug, and maintain a solid database-driven app using both SQL and .NET.

Setting up SQL Server Express

Up until now, we have been working with in-memory data, quick to use, but lost every time we restart the app. Now, by setting up SQL Server Express, we will give Trackr a permanent home for our tasks, allowing us to store, retrieve, and manipulate data in a way that scales as our needs grow. The SQL Server Express is Microsoft's free, developer-friendly version of their enterprise database platform, making it the perfect partner for our journey.

Installing SQL Server Express

We are often faced with many choices for databases, but SQL Server Express stands out for several reasons. It is free, runs smoothly on Windows, and integrates perfectly with .NET applications. We get the full relational power of SQL Server, tables, queries, views, and relationships, but in a form that is easy to set up, light on system resources, and robust enough for real-world learning and small business apps.

To get started, we will download the latest SQL Server Express installer from the official Microsoft site. We will search for ***SQL Server Express download*** or go directly to Microsoft's SQL Server download page. We will find the section for SQL Server Express (for example, SQL Server 2022 Express) and click ***Download***. Once the installer is ready, we run it and choose the ***Basic*** installation. This gives us a quick setup, default options, and a reliable experience. The process usually takes several minutes. The installer will show us the instance name (usually **SQLEXPRESS**) at the end, which we will need when connecting.

Setting up SQL Server Management Studio (SSMS)

Microsoft provides ***SQL Server Management Studio (SSMS)***, which is free and purpose-built for SQL Server databases. We can download it by searching for ***SSMS download*** or by following the link provided in the SQL Server installer's summary.

After downloading, we can easily install and launch SSMS. When the Connect to Server window appears, we use these options:

- ***Server type:*** Database Engine
- ***Server name:*** **`localhost\SQLEXPRESS`** (or sometimes just **`.\SQLEXPRESS`**)
- ***Authentication:*** Windows Authentication

After this, we then click ***Connect***, and we are in.

Creating New Database and Simple Query

After this, we are ready to give Trackr its own database. In SSMS, we expand the server node in Object Explorer, right-click ***Databases***, and select ***New Database***. We enter the name **`TrackrDb`** and click ***OK***. Instantly, SQL Server creates a new, empty database just for us.

If we expand the new **`TrackrDb`**, we see folders for tables, views, and more. For now, it is empty, but this is where we will soon design and store Trackr's data.

After this, with **`TrackrDb`** highlighted, we then click ***New Query*** in the toolbar. In the query window, we type:

```
SELECT 'Trackr is ready for data!' AS Message;
```

Here, we click ***Execute*** (or press F5). If we see a result grid with our message, we have successfully connected and can run SQL commands. Our Trackr app now has a professional, persistent foundation.

In the following, I will quickly brief you about what makes a relational database special:

- ***Tables*** let us store many types of data, each with a clear structure, just like spreadsheets, but much more powerful.
- ***Rows*** are the actual data entries, each task will become a row.
- ***Columns*** describe the properties of each entry, Title, DueDate, IsCompleted, and more.
- ***Primary keys*** uniquely identify each row, which makes updates and deletes reliable.
- ***Relationships*** let us connect tables, later, we might relate tasks to users, categories, or projects.

This way of organizing data is robust and scalable. As Trackr grows, we can add features and link different pieces of data together without fear of losing control.

In the next steps, we will use this foundation to create tables, connect our .NET application, and experience firsthand what it means to work with persistent, relational data in a real-world setting. And then, we will design a schema for our tasks, see how Entity Framework Core bridges C# and SQL, and unlock querying, searching, and updating in ways we could never do with in-memory lists.

Designing Tables for Tasks and Related Entities

In tis topic, we will design the core tables for Trackr and we will do this directly inside SQL Server Management Studio (SSMS), using both the visual designer and SQL queries. We will not just create a tasks table; we will also consider optional related entities such as categories and users, learning how to apply primary keys and foreign keys so our data is relational and well-structured.

Creating Tasks Table

To start with, we will build the heart of Trackr, our Tasks table. This table will store every task's key detail, such as, an ID, title, description, status, due date, and (optionally) references to a user or category.

To do this, we will go to SSMS, right-click on "Tables" under TrackrDb and select "New Table…"

```
CREATE TABLE Tasks (
    TaskId INT IDENTITY(1,1) PRIMARY KEY,
    Title NVARCHAR(100) NOT NULL,
    Description NVARCHAR(500) NULL,
    Status NVARCHAR(50) NOT NULL DEFAULT 'Pending',
    DueDate DATE NULL,
    CategoryId INT NULL,
    UserId INT NULL
);
```

Here, the:

- **`TaskId`** is the ***primary key***, automatically incrementing for each new task.
- **`Title`** and **`Status`** are required. **`Description`** and **`DueDate`** are optional.

- **`CategoryId`** and **`UserId`** will become ***foreign keys*** to other tables if we decide to link tasks to categories or users.

After this, we then click ***Execute*** to create the table.

Designing Categories Table

The categories allow us to group tasks, filter them, and add color to our app. Let us create a simple Categories table:

```
CREATE TABLE Categories (
    CategoryId INT IDENTITY(1,1) PRIMARY KEY,
    Name NVARCHAR(50) NOT NULL,
    Color NVARCHAR(20) NULL
);
```

Each category has a unique **`CategoryId`** (primary key), a required name, and an optional color (such as "Red", "Blue", "Green").

Designing Users Table

If we want to assign tasks to users, we need to build a users table. This could grow to support authentication later:

```
CREATE TABLE Users (
    UserId INT IDENTITY(1,1) PRIMARY KEY,
    UserName NVARCHAR(50) NOT NULL,
    Email NVARCHAR(100) NOT NULL,
    CreatedAt DATETIME NOT NULL DEFAULT GETDATE()
);
```

Here, the **`UserId`** is the primary key. The **`UserName`** and **`Email`** are required for every user. We do also capture the account creation time.

Adding Foreign Keys

Now that we have supporting tables, we can now link our Tasks to Categories and Users using ***foreign keys***. This will guarantee that every referenced category or user actually exists in the corresponding table.

```
ALTER TABLE Tasks
ADD CONSTRAINT FK_Tasks_Categories
    FOREIGN KEY (CategoryId) REFERENCES
Categories(CategoryId);
ALTER TABLE Tasks
ADD CONSTRAINT FK_Tasks_Users
    FOREIGN KEY (UserId) REFERENCES Users(UserId);
```

These statements ensure that any value placed in **CategoryId** or **UserId** in the Tasks table must exist in the Categories or Users table. If someone tries to assign a task to a non-existent user, the database will reject it, keeping our data clean.

Inserting Task with Relationships

We will now insert a sample category and user, and then create a new task that references both:

```
INSERT INTO Categories (Name, Color) VALUES ('Work', 'Blue');
INSERT INTO Users (UserName, Email) VALUES ('alice',
'alice@example.com');
-- Now use the new IDs to create a task
INSERT INTO Tasks (Title, Status, DueDate, CategoryId, UserId)
VALUES ('Prepare project report', 'Pending', '2026-02-01', 1,
1);
```

After this, we can then run:

```
SELECT * FROM Tasks;
```

With this, we should see our new task, with references to the correct category and user. If we try to use an invalid **CategoryId** or **UserId**, it will result in an error, thus proving our relationships are enforced. In the next topics, we will learn how to connect our .NET app to this schema and start building true database-driven features together.

Writing Core SQL for Task Domain

To start with:

Inserting New Tasks

We will begin by adding a new task to the **Tasks** table. We will include references to a user and category, assuming we have valid IDs from our previous inserts.

```
INSERT INTO Tasks (Title, Description, Status, DueDate, CategoryId, UserId)
VALUES (
    'Write SQL Documentation',
    'Draft and review the SQL help files for Trackr.',
    'Pending',
    '2026-03-01',
    1,  -- Existing CategoryId, e.g., "Work"
    2   -- Existing UserId, e.g., "alice"
);
```

If we want to insert a task without a user or category, simply use **NULL** for those fields.

Selecting Tasks

To list all tasks, we can use a straightforward **SELECT**:

```
SELECT * FROM Tasks;
```

And, if we want to get only the essential details:

```
SELECT TaskId, Title, Status, DueDate FROM Tasks;
```

If we want to fetch tasks that are still pending:

```
SELECT TaskId, Title, DueDate
FROM Tasks
WHERE Status = 'Pending';
```

Joining Tasks to Related Tables

When we want to show richer information, like the category name or the user assigned, we can then use **JOIN** statements.

In the following, we can see tasks with their category names and user names:

```
SELECT
    T.TaskId,
    T.Title,
    T.Status,
    T.DueDate,
    C.Name AS CategoryName,
    U.UserName AS AssignedTo
FROM
    Tasks T
    LEFT JOIN Categories C ON T.CategoryId = C.CategoryId
    LEFT JOIN Users U ON T.UserId = U.UserId;
```

Here, the **LEFT JOIN** means every task is listed, even if it has no category or user assigned. We can filter further if needed, for example, to see only tasks assigned to a specific user:

```
SELECT T.TaskId, T.Title, T.Status
FROM Tasks T
INNER JOIN Users U ON T.UserId = U.UserId
WHERE U.UserName = 'alice';
```

Updating Tasks

Suppose we want to mark a task as completed and update the status:

```
UPDATE Tasks
SET Status = 'Completed'
WHERE TaskId = 3;
```

Or, if we want to reassign a task to another user and set a new due date:

```
UPDATE Tasks
SET UserId = 2, DueDate = '2026-03-15'
```

```
WHERE TaskId = 5;
```

Deleting Tasks

To remove a task by its ID:

```
DELETE FROM Tasks
WHERE TaskId = 7;
```

But here, be careful, the deletes are permanent unless we implement soft deletes (e.g., marking a status as "Archived").

Combining Filtering, Sorting, and Limits

And, if we want to see the five most urgent, pending tasks, sorted by due date:

```
SELECT TaskId, Title, DueDate
FROM Tasks
WHERE Status = 'Pending'
ORDER BY DueDate ASC
OFFSET 0 ROWS FETCH NEXT 5 ROWS ONLY;
```

This is helpful for dashboards or paging through results.

With all these skills, we can support the Trackr as it scales, and can aim to bring professional SQL habits into every project we touch.

Transactions and Integrity Constraints

Do you know that transactions let us group several SQL operations into a single, all-or-nothing unit, so if one part fails, everything rolls back, ensuring data stays consistent. And, the integrity constraints are rules at the database level (like requiring unique values or valid foreign keys) that automatically enforce correctness, so even if bugs slip into our code, the database protects us from invalid data.

In the following, we will practice these features, which will give us real-world skills for reliable, safe data operations.

Wrapping Multiple Operations Inside Transaction

So here, let us say that we want to insert a new category, add a new user, and assign a new task to both, all at once. And, we want these operations to either all succeed, or if one fails, none of them should happen.

For this, within SSMS, we will open a new query window and write:

```
BEGIN TRANSACTION;
BEGIN TRY
    INSERT INTO Categories (Name, Color) VALUES ('Home',
'Green');
    INSERT INTO Users (UserName, Email) VALUES ('bob',
'bob@example.com');

    -- Suppose the new category gets ID 2 and the user gets ID
2
    INSERT INTO Tasks (Title, Status, DueDate, CategoryId,
UserId)
    VALUES ('Fix kitchen light', 'Pending', '2026-03-10', 2,
2);
    COMMIT TRANSACTION;
END TRY
BEGIN CATCH
    ROLLBACK TRANSACTION;
    SELECT ERROR_MESSAGE() AS ErrorMessage;
END CATCH
```

From the above, if all inserts succeed, we ***commit*** and changes are saved. And, if any insert fails (for example, if the task references a non-existent user), the entire group is ***rolled back***, leaving the database unchanged.

Working with Integrity Constraints

The integrity constraints enforce rules such as:

- Every task must have a unique primary key.
- Foreign keys must point to valid, existing rows.
- Some fields cannot be null or empty.

In the following, we will review and create these constraints practically.

Primary Key and Not Null Constraints

When we created our tables, we specified primary keys and NOT NULL fields:

```
CREATE TABLE Tasks (
    TaskId INT IDENTITY(1,1) PRIMARY KEY,
    Title NVARCHAR(100) NOT NULL,
    Status NVARCHAR(50) NOT NULL DEFAULT 'Pending',
    ...
);
```

If we try to insert a task without a Title or with a duplicate TaskId, SQL Server will reject it.

Foreign Key Constraints

The foreign keys make sure any referenced category or user exists. For example, this fails:

```
INSERT INTO Tasks (Title, Status, CategoryId)
VALUES ('Bad task', 'Pending', 999);  -- 999 does not exist in
Categories
```

The SQL Server will stop and display an error, keeping our data safe from "orphaned" rows.

Unique Constraints

And, suppose if we want each category name to be unique:

```
ALTER TABLE Categories
ADD CONSTRAINT UQ_Categories_Name UNIQUE (Name);
```

With it, the inserting of two categories named "Work" will trigger an error.

Observing Database Enforcement

Let us deliberately trigger some constraint violations to see how SQL Server protects us.

For example, if we try to insert a task with a missing required field:

```
INSERT INTO Tasks (Status)
```

```
VALUES ('Pending');  -- Missing Title (NOT NULL)
```

The expected result is that the SQL Server rejects the insert and reports "Cannot insert the value NULL into column 'Title'..."

And, let us say that you are trying to delete a category in use:

```
DELETE FROM Categories WHERE CategoryId = 1;
```

So here, if any tasks reference this category, the database will block the deletion because of the foreign key constraint. This avoids breaking the relationship.

Our approach here, as shown above, is to wrap our operations in transactions and use strong constraints, which helps us develop habits for building reliable, auditable, and self-correcting applications, even when things go wrong.

Connecting ADO.NET from Console Utility

We will now build a practical bridge between our Trackr database and C# by writing a simple console utility that uses ***ADO.NET***, the foundational data access technology for .NET. With ADO.NET, we can connect directly to SQL Server Express, send SQL queries or commands, and process results row by row.

So here in this topic, we will make use of **SqlConnection**, **SqlCommand**, and **SqlDataReader**, seeing each one in action. It will teach us to debug, automate, or script the database interactions without relying on higher-level ORMs.

Setting up Project

To start with, we will first create a new C# console app using the terminal:

```
dotnet new console -n TrackrDbUtility
cd TrackrDbUtility
```

Next, we will add the **System.Data.SqlClient** package if it is not already available:

```
dotnet add package System.Data.SqlClient
```

Crafting Connection String

After this, we need a connection string to tell ADO.NET how to find our SQL Server Express instance and which database to use.

For our development environment, it looks like this:

```
string connectionString =
@"Server=localhost\SQLEXPRESS;Database=TrackrDb;Trusted_Connec
tion=True;";
```

Writing Core Utility

We will now write a simple program that:

- Connects to SQL Server Express
- Inserts a new task
- Reads and displays all tasks

Following is how we do it step by step in **`Program.cs`**:

```
using System;
using System.Data.SqlClient;
class Program
{
    static void Main()
    {
        string connectionString =
@"Server=localhost\SQLEXPRESS;Database=TrackrDb;Trusted_Connec
tion=True;";
        using (var connection = new
SqlConnection(connectionString))
        {
            connection.Open();
            // Insert a new task
            string insertSql = "INSERT INTO Tasks (Title,
Status) VALUES (@title, @status);";
            using (var insertCmd = new SqlCommand(insertSql,
connection))
            {
                insertCmd.Parameters.AddWithValue("@title",
"ADO.NET Demo Task");
```

```
                insertCmd.Parameters.AddWithValue("@status",
"Pending");
                int rowsInserted =
insertCmd.ExecuteNonQuery();
                Console.WriteLine($"{rowsInserted} task(s)
inserted.");
            }
            // Read all tasks
            string selectSql = "SELECT TaskId, Title, Status
FROM Tasks;";
            using (var selectCmd = new SqlCommand(selectSql,
connection))
            using (var reader = selectCmd.ExecuteReader())
            {
                Console.WriteLine("Current Tasks:");
                while (reader.Read())
                {
                    int id = reader.GetInt32(0);
                    string title = reader.GetString(1);
                    string status = reader.GetString(2);
                    Console.WriteLine($"  {id}: {title}
[{status}]");
                }
            }
        }
    }
}
```

The ADO.NET contains following components:

- ***SqlConnection*** which manages the physical connection to SQL Server. We open and close it inside a **`using`** block for safety.
- ***SqlCommand*** represents a SQL statement to execute. We use parameterized queries to

prevent SQL injection and handle dynamic data.

- ***SqlDataReader*** reads rows returned from a **SELECT** query. We iterate through results, accessing column values by index or name.

Running and Observing Utility

Next, when we run our console app (**dotnet run**), it should show:

```
1 task(s) inserted.
Current Tasks:
  1: Prepare project report [Pending]
  2: ADO.NET Demo Task [Pending]
```

So here, every time we run the program, it inserts a new demo task and prints out the current list of tasks in the database.

Updating and Deleting Tasks

Nowlet us say that if we want to update a task:

```
string updateSql = "UPDATE Tasks SET Status = @status WHERE
TaskId = @id;";
using (var updateCmd = new SqlCommand(updateSql, connection))
{
    updateCmd.Parameters.AddWithValue("@status", "Completed");
    updateCmd.Parameters.AddWithValue("@id", 2);
    int rowsUpdated = updateCmd.ExecuteNonQuery();
    Console.WriteLine($"{rowsUpdated} task(s) updated.");
}
```

And, if we want to delete a task:

```
string deleteSql = "DELETE FROM Tasks WHERE TaskId = @id;";
using (var deleteCmd = new SqlCommand(deleteSql, connection))
{
    deleteCmd.Parameters.AddWithValue("@id", 2);
```

```
    int rowsDeleted = deleteCmd.ExecuteNonQuery();
    Console.WriteLine($"{rowsDeleted} task(s) deleted.");
}
```

With this, we saw each step, connecting, sending commands, reading results, and closing resources, so we can troubleshoot, automate, or debug issues at the lowest level. This console utility serves as a diagnostic tool for seeding data, verifying schema changes, or performing manual maintenance outside the main Trackr application.

Summary

During this chapter, we built a solid foundation for persistent, relational data in our Trackr application by working step by step with SQL Server Express. We began with a clear introduction to SQL Server Express, learning how to install it, connect with SQL Server Management Studio, and create a new dedicated database for our project. We then moved on to designing tables that reflect our task domain, applying primary keys and setting up foreign keys to support future relationships with categories and users. By practicing direct SQL, we wrote queries to insert, update, delete, and select tasks, including joins to pull together information from related tables. We wrapped our operations in transactions, learned how integrity constraints such as primary keys and unique or foreign key constraints enforce data quality, and deliberately tested these features by observing the database's protective behaviors in action. Finally, we bridged our application code with the database using ADO.NET, writing a console utility that connects, inserts, updates, and reads data using raw SQL and essential classes like SqlConnection, SqlCommand, and SqlDataReader. These skills gave us confidence in both database structure and data access, preparing us for robust application development and deeper troubleshooting.

Chapter 8: Working with Entity Framework Core

Overview

In this chapter, we're going to learn how to connect the dots between the .NET code and a real SQL Server database using Entity Framework Core. To start, we'll design entity classes that closely match our Trackr schema, and then we'll create a **`DbContext`** to manage database connections and operations. Then, we'll dive into data annotations and Fluent API configuration, giving us the power to enforce business rules, define relationships, and control how the models map to database tables. Along the way, we'll create and apply migrations to make sure the database schema always matches up with the evolving requirements.

And, we'll be using LINQ for querying, which is expressive and type-safe. We'll also learn how to inspect the SQL statements that are generated behind the scenes for debugging and optimization. By the time we're done, we'll have a handle on the workflow for building, maintaining, and querying a database-driven .NET app, which will set us up for advanced data access and application features in Trackr or any future project.

DbContext and Entity Classes

The Entity Framework Core is the modern, open-source ORM (Object-Relational Mapper) for .NET. Instead of writing SQL for every operation, the EF Core lets us work with data as strongly-typed C# objects, saving, querying, and updating with LINQ. It handles translating our code into SQL behind the scenes. It allows us to focus on our domain model, our tasks, categories, and users, without losing touch with how data is stored and related in SQL Server.

In the following, we will explore the process of setting up EF Core, and we will focus only on what is necessary to get our entity classes mapped to the database and to get our **`TaskDbContext`** working with SQL Server Express.

Add EF Core Packages

To start with, we will add three packages:

```
dotnet add package Microsoft.EntityFrameworkCore
dotnet add package Microsoft.EntityFrameworkCore.SqlServer
dotnet add package Microsoft.EntityFrameworkCore.Tools
```

It gives our project all the tools to talk to SQL Server using EF Core.

Create Simple Entity Classes

We will now create one C# class for each table such as Task, Category, and User.

- TaskItem.cs

```
public class TaskItem
{
    public int TaskId { get; set; }         // Primary key,
matches TaskId in SQL
    public string Title { get; set; }
    public string Status { get; set; }
    public DateTime? DueDate { get; set; }
    // Optional: Link to category and user (foreign keys)
    public int? CategoryId { get; set; }
    public Category Category { get; set; }
    public int? UserId { get; set; }
    public User User { get; set; }
}
```

- Category.cs

```
public class Category
{
    public int CategoryId { get; set; }    // Primary key
    public string Name { get; set; }
    public ICollection<TaskItem> Tasks { get; set; }
}
```

- User.cs

```
public class User
{
    public int UserId { get; set; }          // Primary key
    public string UserName { get; set; }
    public ICollection<TaskItem> Tasks { get; set; }
}
```

If we prefer, we can skip navigation properties (like **`Category`** or **`Tasks`**) at first, and add them once we see the code running.

Create TaskDbContex

This class connects everything together and tells EF Core how to find our database, as shown below:

```
using Microsoft.EntityFrameworkCore;

public class TaskDbContext : DbContext

{

    public DbSet<TaskItem> Tasks { get; set; }

    public DbSet<Category> Categories { get; set; }

    public DbSet<User> Users { get; set; }

    protected override void
OnConfiguring(DbContextOptionsBuilder optionsBuilder)

    {

        // This must match the actual SQL Server Express
setup!

optionsBuilder.UseSqlServer(@"Server=localhost\SQLEXPRESS;Data
base=TrackrDb;Trusted_Connection=True;");

    }

}
```

This one file does almost all the work for setup!

EF Core now knows about our tables and where to find the database.

Connecting and Inserting Data

We will now check that everything works by adding a few lines in **Program.cs**:

```
class Program

{

    static void Main()

    {

        using (var db = new TaskDbContext())
```

```
        {
            // Add a new category
            var cat = new Category { Name = "Learning" };
            db.Categories.Add(cat);
            db.SaveChanges();
            // Add a new task using that category
            var task = new TaskItem
            {
                Title = "Try EF Core basics",
                Status = "Pending",
                DueDate = DateTime.Today.AddDays(7),
                CategoryId = cat.CategoryId
            };
            db.Tasks.Add(task);
            db.SaveChanges();
            // Read all tasks and print
            foreach (var t in db.Tasks)
            {
                Console.WriteLine($"{t.TaskId}: {t.Title}
[{t.Status}]");
            }
        }
    }
}
```

When we run this (**dotnet run**), the EF Core will insert our data into SQL Server and print every task in the database.

Now, any time we need to add, update, or read data, we work with C# objects, and EF Core translates everything for us behind the scenes.

Configuring Mappings and Relationships

We begin by making our C# classes match the business rules we want to enforce in SQL Server. Data annotations are direct and keep everything readable in the class itself.

Data Annotations

For this, we will consider our **TaskItem** to learn this topic. In this, we will add just enough attributes to mirror the constraints we already expect from our database.

```
using System.ComponentModel.DataAnnotations;
using System.ComponentModel.DataAnnotations.Schema;
public class TaskItem
{
    [Key]
    public int TaskId { get; set; }
    [Required]
    [StringLength(100)]
    public string Title { get; set; }
    [StringLength(500)]
    public string Description { get; set; }
    [Required]
    [StringLength(50)]
    public string Status { get; set; } = "Pending";
    public DateTime? DueDate { get; set; }
    public int? CategoryId { get; set; }
    [ForeignKey(nameof(CategoryId))]
    public Category Category { get; set; }
    public int? UserId { get; set; }
    [ForeignKey(nameof(UserId))]
    public User User { get; set; }
}
```

As we annotate, we will notice how we have spelled out what must exist (**[Required]**), what has limits (**[StringLength]**), and what links to other entities (**[ForeignKey]**). After this, the EF Core will enforce the right schema and validation rules when it creates or updates the database. If we try to save a task with no title, our code will raise an error before anything reaches the database.

Now, as taught above, we will do the same for **Category** and **User**:

```
public class Category
{
    [Key]
    public int CategoryId { get; set; }
    [Required]
    [StringLength(50)]
    public string Name { get; set; }
    [StringLength(20)]
    public string Color { get; set; }
    public ICollection<TaskItem> Tasks { get; set; }
}
public class User
{
    [Key]
    public int UserId { get; set; }
    [Required]
    [StringLength(50)]
    public string UserName { get; set; }
    [StringLength(100)]
    public string Email { get; set; }
    public ICollection<TaskItem> Tasks { get; set; }
}
```

With data annotations alone, we can set up most of the key rules for our model.

More Control wtith Fluent API

Now, as we advance, there are times when data annotations are not enough, perhaps we want to make a property unique, set up a composite key, or define exactly what happens when a category is deleted. That is where the Fluent API comes in.

In the following, we will do all Fluent API configuration in the **`OnModelCreating`** method of **`TaskDbContext`**.

```
protected override void OnModelCreating(ModelBuilder
modelBuilder)
{
    // Configure TaskItem relationships and property rules
    modelBuilder.Entity<TaskItem>(entity =>
    {
        entity.Property(t => t.Title)
            .IsRequired()
            .HasMaxLength(100);
        entity.Property(t => t.Status)
            .IsRequired()
            .HasMaxLength(50)
            .HasDefaultValue("Pending");
        entity.HasOne(t => t.Category)
            .WithMany(c => c.Tasks)
            .HasForeignKey(t => t.CategoryId)
            .OnDelete(DeleteBehavior.SetNull);
        entity.HasOne(t => t.User)
            .WithMany(u => u.Tasks)
            .HasForeignKey(t => t.UserId)
            .OnDelete(DeleteBehavior.SetNull);
    });
    // Make category names unique
    modelBuilder.Entity<Category>(entity =>
```

```
    {
        entity.HasIndex(c => c.Name).IsUnique();
    });
}
```

Now here in the above, you must notice what is happening in real time:

- The use of **`.OnDelete(DeleteBehavior.SetNull)`** ensures that if a category or user is deleted, the tasks linked to them are not lost, rather their link is simply set to null.
- Also, if we add **`.HasIndex(c => c.Name).IsUnique()`**, it helps to prevent duplicate category names. If anyone tries to save two "Work" categories, they will see an error.

If we want to add even more advanced rules, like composite keys or custom column names, the Fluent API will handle that too, all in the same method.

Let us imagine saving a new task with a very long title or a missing required field. The EF Core will stop us and show an error. If we try to add a duplicate category, we get a friendly complaint, not a corrupted database. If we delete a category, any tasks assigned to it simply lose their category assignment, but remain in our system.

With data annotations and Fluent API rules set up like this, we give Trackr clear business logic and database-level safety. This keeps our code and data in sync, makes our rules obvious to anyone reading the code, and makes our next feature or refactor much safer. Whenever we want to confirm how our data will behave, we always know where to check, and Trackr will get better with every update.

Creating and Applying Migrations

The igrations allow us to keep our database schema in sync with our C# classes as we add features or change business rules. In this topic, we will see how to create our very first migration, apply it to build the actual tables, and then make a small change to one of our properties and create a follow-up migration to handle that update. We will see every command, the reasoning behind each step, and what happens both in the code and in the database.

Creating Initial Migration

Before we begin with, we must ensure that the Trackr project has the EF Core Tools package installed. If not, then we shall add it:

```
dotnet add package Microsoft.EntityFrameworkCore.Tools
```

After this, we will then open the terminal in our project directory and run the following command to create an initial migration:

```
dotnet ef migrations add InitialCreate
```

This command generates a folder called **Migrations** and places a new C# file inside it. The file contains all the SQL instructions needed to create tables, columns, keys, and relationships based on our current entity classes and DbContext configuration.

Applying Migration to Generate DB Schema

So here, we will apply this migration to our SQL Server Express database. We will use the update command as below:

```
dotnet ef database update
```

With this, the EF Core connects to the database specified in our **TaskDbContext** and executes the migration, creating all the tables, columns, indexes, and relationships as per our entity definitions and configuration (both data annotations and Fluent API).

If we open SQL Server Management Studio and refresh our TrackrDb, we will now see the actual tables (**Tasks**, **Categories**, **Users**), all with the correct keys, foreign keys, and constraints in place.

Making Change

Here, if we want to allow longer task titles, perhaps increasing the maximum length from 100 to 200 characters, we can easily do it by adding simple edits to our **TaskItem** class:

```
[Required]
[StringLength(200)] // Previously 100
public string Title { get; set; }
```

Creating and Applying Second Migration

Now, we need to tell EF Core about this change and update our database schema accordingly. For this, we simply run:

```
dotnet ef migrations add IncreaseTaskTitleLength
```

By doing this, the EF Core detects the difference between the current database schema and the updated entity classes. It creates a new migration file describing how to alter the **Tasks** table to change the maximum length of the **Title** column.

Here, if we want to apply this migration:

```
dotnet ef database update
```

The change is applied to the database: from now on, **`Title`** in the **`Tasks`** table can store up to 200 characters.

We can also open SSMS and right-click on the **`Tasks`** table, then choose ***Design***. We will see that the **`Title`** column now allows up to 200 characters. If we insert or update a task title with more than 100 but less than or equal to 200 characters, the operation will succeed. By practicing with migrations, it builds a habit of disciplined, professional data management.

Querying LINQ and Inspecting SQL

Here, in this topic, we will learn to use LINQ with EF Core to query data from our Trackr database, and then see how to inspect the exact SQL statements that EF Core generates and sends to SQL Server Express. This will help us to understand both, how LINQ makes querying expressive and type-safe, and how we can optimize or debug by checking the real SQL under the hood.

Querying with LINQ

To start with, we will perform a few queries using the LINQ against our **`DbSet<TaskItem>`**, just as we would in a live project.

Following queries we will run:

Fetch Tasks

```
using (var db = new TaskDbContext())
{
    var allTasks = db.Tasks.ToList();
    foreach (var task in allTasks)
    {
        Console.WriteLine($"{task.TaskId}: {task.Title}
[{task.Status}]");
    }
}
```

This retrieves all tasks from the **`Tasks`** table and prints their details.

Filtering and Ordering Tasks

Suppose we want to get all pending tasks, sorted by due date:

```
using (var db = new TaskDbContext())
{
    var pendingTasks = db.Tasks
        .Where(t => t.Status == "Pending")
        .OrderBy(t => t.DueDate)
        .ToList();
    foreach (var task in pendingTasks)
    {
        Console.WriteLine($"{task.TaskId}: {task.Title} (Due:
{task.DueDate?.ToShortDateString() ?? "None"})");
    }
}
```

Here, the LINQ translates our filtering (**`Where`**) and ordering (**`OrderBy`**) into SQL, which gets executed on the server.

Joining with Related Entities

We will try to load tasks along with their category names, using **`Include`** for eager loading:

```
using Microsoft.EntityFrameworkCore;
using (var db = new TaskDbContext())
{
    var tasksWithCategories = db.Tasks
        .Include(t => t.Category)
        .ToList();
    foreach (var task in tasksWithCategories)
    {
        string category = task.Category?.Name ??
"Uncategorized";
```

```
        Console.WriteLine($"{task.TaskId}: {task.Title}
[{category}]");
    }
}
```

The EF Core fetches both the tasks and their related categories in one go.

Inspecting Generated SQL

Understanding what SQL EF Core actually runs is important for debugging and performance. The EF Core lets us log or capture the SQL behind any LINQ query.

Logging SQL to Console

We will modify **`OnConfiguring`** in **`TaskDbContext`** to log SQL queries:

```
protected override void OnConfiguring(DbContextOptionsBuilder
optionsBuilder)
{
    optionsBuilder

.UseSqlServer(@"Server=localhost\SQLEXPRESS;Database=TrackrDb;
Trusted_Connection=True;")
        .LogTo(Console.WriteLine); // This outputs SQL to the
console
}
```

So here, when we run any query, the actual SQL will be printed to our console. For example, if we run a LINQ query such as **`db.Tasks.Where(t => t.Status == "Pending",)`**, it might produce:

```
SELECT [t].[TaskId], [t].[Title], [t].[Status], [t].[DueDate],
...
FROM [Tasks] AS [t]
WHERE [t].[Status] = N'Pending'
ORDER BY [t].[DueDate]
```

Inspecting SQL in Code

If we want to see the SQL for a query before it runs, we can use the **ToQueryString()** method:

```
using Microsoft.EntityFrameworkCore;
using (var db = new TaskDbContext())
{
    var query = db.Tasks.Where(t => t.Status == "Pending");
    string sql = query.ToQueryString();
    Console.WriteLine(sql);
}
```

This prints the exact SQL statement EF Core would send for that LINQ query, but does not execute it.

Now, with these techniques, we can confidently use LINQ to write expressive queries and always verify how those queries operate on our real Trackr database. This closes the loop between application logic and data storage, and then it gives us complete control and understanding at every level.

Handling Common Pitfalls

We will now put everything together and see how we can use Entity Framework Core to insert, update, and delete entities, and how to avoid common mistakes that can trip up even experienced developers. In the following, we will walk through each operation in code, observe what happens in the database, and troubleshoot classic issues like missing Includes and entity tracking surprises.

Inserting Entities

We begin by adding a new category and a new task to the database.

```
using (var db = new TaskDbContext())
{
    var cat = new Category { Name = "Errands" };
    db.Categories.Add(cat);
    db.SaveChanges();
    var task = new TaskItem
    {
```

```
        Title = "Pick up groceries",
        Status = "Pending",
        CategoryId = cat.CategoryId,
        DueDate = DateTime.Today.AddDays(2)
    };
    db.Tasks.Add(task);
    db.SaveChanges();
    Console.WriteLine("Task added: " + task.Title);
}
```

Here, we create our objects, add them to the appropriate **DbSet**, and call **SaveChanges()** to commit them to the database.

After saving, each object's primary key (**CategoryId**, **TaskId**) will be set automatically.

Updating Entities

Now let us update an existing task, for example, marking it as completed.

```
using (var db = new TaskDbContext())
{
    var task = db.Tasks.FirstOrDefault(t => t.Title == "Pick
up groceries");
    if (task != null)
    {
        task.Status = "Completed";
        db.SaveChanges();
        Console.WriteLine($"Task {task.TaskId} marked as
completed.");
    }
}
```

Form the above, we can fetch the task, change its status, and save again. EF Core tracks changes on entities loaded from the context, so only modified fields are updated.

Deleting Entities

Here, we will try to delete a task by its ID:

```
using (var db = new TaskDbContext())
{
    var task = db.Tasks.FirstOrDefault(t => t.Title == "Pick
up groceries");
    if (task != null)
    {
        db.Tasks.Remove(task);
        db.SaveChanges();
        Console.WriteLine($"Task {task.TaskId} deleted.");
    }
}
```

When we remove an entity and call **SaveChanges()**, EF Core generates the necessary SQL to delete that row from the database.

Tracking Issues

EF Core tracks changes only for entities retrieved in the same **DbContext** instance. If we fetch an entity, close the context, then try to update in a new context, EF Core will not track the changes automatically.

Following is a simple situation:

```
TaskItem task;
using (var db = new TaskDbContext())
{
    task = db.Tasks.First();
}
// The context is now disposed. If we update and try to save,
nothing happens:
task.Status = "Completed";
using (var db = new TaskDbContext())
```

```
{
    db.SaveChanges(); // No update!
}
```

So, in this example, the soluiton is that we need to attach the entity and mark it as modified:

```
using (var db = new TaskDbContext())
{
    db.Tasks.Attach(task);
    task.Status = "Completed";
    db.Entry(task).State = EntityState.Modified;
    db.SaveChanges();
}
```

Missing Includes

There is another situation wherein, if we query related data (like a task's category), the EF Core does not load related entities unless told to do so. If we forget **.Include**, we might get **null** for navigation properties.

Following is a quick sutation:

```
using (var db = new TaskDbContext())
{
    var task = db.Tasks.First();
    Console.WriteLine(task.Category?.Name); // Might print
nothing!
}
```

The possible solution is to use **.Include()** to load the related data:

```
using Microsoft.EntityFrameworkCore;
using (var db = new TaskDbContext())
{
    var task = db.Tasks.Include(t => t.Category).First();
    Console.WriteLine(task.Category?.Name); // Now this works!
```

```
}
```

If we stay aware of these practical steps and common pitfalls, we can make Trackr robust, predictable, and ready for real-world use. This will help us build habits that will benefit us in every .NET data-driven project.

Summary

Throughout this chapter, we gained hands-on experience integrating Entity Framework Core into our Trackr application. We started by building simple entity classes that mapped directly to our SQL Server tables for tasks, categories, and users, ensuring a clear link between our C# models and database structure. We set up the **`TaskDbContext`**, which established the database connection and enabled us to manage all data operations in a consistent way. We learned how to use data annotations for quick, readable configuration right inside our entity classes, and then practiced using the Fluent API within our context to set up relationships, keys, and constraints with more flexibility.

We also wrote LINQ queries to fetch, filter, and join our entities, and used logging tools to inspect the raw SQL that EF Core generated. Finally, we inserted, updated, and deleted entities in the database, while troubleshooting common pitfalls such as missing Includes for navigation properties and tracking issues when entities cross context boundaries. These steps built our confidence to use EF Core for all CRUD operations and gave us habits to keep data and code in sync as our application evolves.

Chapter 9: Building Backend with ASP.NET Core and EF Core

Overview

In this chapter, we will learn how to organize and implement a robust backend architecture for the Trackr application using ASP.NET Core and Entity Framework Core. The chapter will introduce the layered approach, separating the application into controllers, services, and repositories, to ensure every responsibility has a clear place and is easy to manage as the project grows. We will practice implementing repository methods that encapsulate data access, develop services that enforce business logic and validation, and wire these components together using the built-in DI system.

Later, it will walkthrough in defining DTOs (Data Transfer Objects) to maintain a clean separation between the public API and the internal data model, a best practice for secure and future-proof APIs. We will see how to add robust validation, centralize error handling for predictable API responses, and integrate structured logging to support monitoring and troubleshooting. By the end of this chapter, we will have hands-on experience building, organizing, and securing a backend ready for real-world requirements, confident in the ability to maintain and extend Trackr with ease.

Layering Controllers, Services, and Repositories

We'll need to keep making changes to our app because it's not going to stay simple for long. There are more features, business rules change, and sometimes data sources change or grow. When working on a beginner project, it might seem easier to mix all the database calls, validation, and web responses inside a single controller. At first, this might feel fast, but it'll get tricky real fast. The code will get all tangled, and it'll be a pain to test, maintain, or change.

Instead, we can embrace a layered backend. Using it, we can draw a clear line between web interaction, business logic, and data access:

- ***Controller Layer:*** Accepts HTTP requests, validates input, and sends responses. It should not know about business details or database internals.
- ***Service Layer:*** Holds our real "application brain", all the rules, workflows, and cross-entity coordination.
- ***Repository Layer:*** Knows only about storage and retrieval. It hides EF Core, SQL, and any future data source changes.

Such structure can give us three powerful advantages:

- Any rule or feature is easy to find and update.
- Each layer is easy to test in isolation.
- The system can evolve, add logging, switch databases, or automate workflows, without chaos.

With that in mind, we can then roll up our sleeves and shape each layer for Trackr.

Creating Repository Layer

We've got a special place for the repository layer where we manage all the interactions with EF Core and SQL Server. When we hide these details behind a simple interface, the rest of our system becomes immune to low-level changes.

To get started, first we need to define the contract for what this repository will provide:

```
public interface ITaskRepository
{
    Task<TaskItem> GetByIdAsync(int id);
    Task<List<TaskItem>> GetAllAsync();
    Task AddAsync(TaskItem task);
    Task UpdateAsync(TaskItem task);
    Task DeleteAsync(int id);
}
```

With it, every method is asynchronous, matching real-world web and database workloads.

Now, we will implement the contract using EF Core in a concrete repository:

```
public class TaskRepository : ITaskRepository
{
    private readonly TaskDbContext _context;
    public TaskRepository(TaskDbContext context)
    {
        _context = context;
    }
    public async Task<TaskItem> GetByIdAsync(int id)
    {
        return await _context.Tasks
            .Include(t => t.Category)
            .Include(t => t.User)
```

```
            .FirstOrDefaultAsync(t => t.TaskId == id);
    }
    public async Task<List<TaskItem>> GetAllAsync()
    {
        return await _context.Tasks
            .Include(t => t.Category)
            .Include(t => t.User)
            .ToListAsync();
    }
    public async Task AddAsync(TaskItem task)
    {
        await _context.Tasks.AddAsync(task);
        await _context.SaveChangesAsync();
    }
    public async Task UpdateAsync(TaskItem task)
    {
        _context.Tasks.Update(task);
        await _context.SaveChangesAsync();
    }
    public async Task DeleteAsync(int id)
    {
        var task = await _context.Tasks.FindAsync(id);
        if (task != null)
        {
            _context.Tasks.Remove(task);
            await _context.SaveChangesAsync();
        }
    }
}
```

The repository now becomes our safe, single source for data access. Every query and update flows through here, keeping data logic out of controllers and services.

Developing Service Layer

The business rules are often more complex than "save this" or "get that." The service layer lets us:

- Validate business logic before data is touched.
- Apply rules (for example, defaulting statuses, preventing duplicate tasks, handling notifications).
- Compose multi-step workflows.

So here, we will first define the service interface:

```
public interface ITaskService
{
    Task<TaskItem> GetTaskAsync(int id);
    Task<List<TaskItem>> ListTasksAsync();
    Task<TaskItem> CreateTaskAsync(TaskItem task);
    Task<bool> UpdateTaskAsync(TaskItem task);
    Task<bool> DeleteTaskAsync(int id);
}
```

And then, we will implement it using our repository:

```
public class TaskService : ITaskService
{
    private readonly ITaskRepository _repository;
    public TaskService(ITaskRepository repository)
    {
        _repository = repository;
    }
    public async Task<TaskItem> GetTaskAsync(int id)
    {
        return await _repository.GetByIdAsync(id);
```

```
    }
    public async Task<List<TaskItem>> ListTasksAsync()
    {
        return await _repository.GetAllAsync();
    }
    public async Task<TaskItem> CreateTaskAsync(TaskItem task)
    {
        // Business logic: set the initial status for every
new task
        task.Status = "Pending";
        await _repository.AddAsync(task);
        return task;
    }
    public async Task<bool> UpdateTaskAsync(TaskItem task)
    {
        var existing = await
_repository.GetByIdAsync(task.TaskId);
        if (existing == null) return false;
        existing.Title = task.Title;
        existing.Status = task.Status;
        existing.DueDate = task.DueDate;
        existing.CategoryId = task.CategoryId;
        await _repository.UpdateAsync(existing);
        return true;
    }
    public async Task<bool> DeleteTaskAsync(int id)
    {
        var existing = await _repository.GetByIdAsync(id);
        if (existing == null) return false;
        await _repository.DeleteAsync(id);
```

```
        return true;
    }
}
```

Here, the service can grow, adding logic for auditing, logging, or integrating with other modules, without affecting our data or web layers.

Building Controller Layer

The controllers turn HTTP requests into clear, predictable responses. They do not know about SQL, and they do not handle deep business logic. They simply:

- Accept incoming requests and user input.
- Call the service layer to handle operations.
- Return HTTP responses.

Given below is a minimal but complete TasksController:

```
[ApiController]
[Route("api/[controller]")]
public class TasksController : ControllerBase
{
    private readonly ITaskService _service;
    public TasksController(ITaskService service)
    {
        _service = service;
    }
    [HttpGet("{id}")]
    public async Task<IActionResult> GetTask(int id)
    {
        var task = await _service.GetTaskAsync(id);
        if (task == null)
            return NotFound();
        return Ok(task);
    }
```

```
    [HttpGet]
    public async Task<IActionResult> GetTasks()
    {
        var tasks = await _service.ListTasksAsync();
        return Ok(tasks);
    }
    [HttpPost]
    public async Task<IActionResult> CreateTask(TaskItem task)
    {
        var created = await _service.CreateTaskAsync(task);
        return CreatedAtAction(nameof(GetTask), new { id =
created.TaskId }, created);
    }
    [HttpPut("{id}")]
    public async Task<IActionResult> UpdateTask(int id,
TaskItem task)
    {
        task.TaskId = id;
        var success = await _service.UpdateTaskAsync(task);
        if (!success)
            return NotFound();
        return NoContent();
    }
    [HttpDelete("{id}")]
    public async Task<IActionResult> DeleteTask(int id)
    {
        var success = await _service.DeleteTaskAsync(id);
        if (!success)
            return NotFound();
        return NoContent();
```

```
    }
}
```

This controller receives only validated, ready-to-process requests, hands them off, and formats the result for the API client.

Registering Layers with DI

We will then finalize by wiring everything in **`Program.cs`**:

```
builder.Services.AddDbContext<TaskDbContext>();
builder.Services.AddScoped<ITaskRepository, TaskRepository>();
builder.Services.AddScoped<ITaskService, TaskService>();
```

With this setup, the ASP.NET Core will automatically connect each piece. Every HTTP request gets a fresh, safe context.

This whole layered design lets us build, debug, and grow Trackr with clarity and confidence, while always knowing exactly where to look for every rule, feature, or bug.

Implementing Repository Methods

We will now work through the actual implementation of our repository methods for tasks in Trackr. Here, we will use EF Core for all database operations, ensuring each method is clean, focused, and hides the database details from the service and controller layers.

Setting up Task Repository Interface

To start with, we will first recap the interface so that each method has a clear, single responsibility:

```
public interface ITaskRepository
{
    Task<TaskItem> GetByIdAsync(int id);
    Task<List<TaskItem>> GetAllAsync();
    Task AddAsync(TaskItem task);
    Task UpdateAsync(TaskItem task);
    Task DeleteAsync(int id);
}
```

Fetching All Tasks

This method should retrieve all tasks from the database, including their categories and users for full context.

```
public async Task<List<TaskItem>> GetAllAsync()
{
    return await _context.Tasks
        .Include(t => t.Category)
        .Include(t => t.User)
        .ToListAsync();
}
```

Here, **`.Include()`** brings in related data. And, the **`.ToListAsync()`** executes the query and returns all results as a list.

Finding Task by ID

We often need a single task with all details. So here, we will use **`FirstOrDefaultAsync`** to fetch one task, or **`null`** if not found.

```
public async Task<TaskItem> GetByIdAsync(int id)
{
    return await _context.Tasks
        .Include(t => t.Category)
        .Include(t => t.User)
        .FirstOrDefaultAsync(t => t.TaskId == id);
}
```

This ensures every lookup by ID also loads related entities. If no match is found, **`null`** is returned.

Adding New Task

We can also add the task entity, then call **`SaveChangesAsync`** to persist it.

```
public async Task AddAsync(TaskItem task)
```

```
{
    await _context.Tasks.AddAsync(task);
    await _context.SaveChangesAsync();
}
```

After this method runs, the new task is stored in the database and its **TaskId** is set.

Updating an Existing Task

For updates, we can attach the modified entity and save.

```
public async Task UpdateAsync(TaskItem task)
{
    _context.Tasks.Update(task);
    await _context.SaveChangesAsync();
}
```

The EF Core tracks which fields changed and generates the correct SQL **UPDATE** statement.

Deleting a Task

We can also fetch by ID to confirm the task exists, then remove and save.

```
public async Task DeleteAsync(int id)
{
    var task = await _context.Tasks.FindAsync(id);
    if (task != null)
    {
        _context.Tasks.Remove(task);
        await _context.SaveChangesAsync();
    }
}
```

If the task does not exist, nothing happens; if it does, it is deleted.

After implementing these methods in **TaskRepository**, the service layer (and by extension, controllers) can interact with tasks in a completely database-agnostic way. If we ever swap out EF

Core for another data provider, or add new storage rules, only the repository code changes, never the logic or API endpoints.

This clear structure also makes it easy to expand, test, or optimize every part of the data workflow in Trackr. If we want to see advanced repository patterns, or add more querying capabilities, we can build on this strong foundation in upcoming topics.

Wiring Services and Repositories through DI

We now move on to connect all our backend layers in Trackr. We must remember that the DI is at the core of modern .NET applications, making it easy to manage dependencies, switch implementations for testing, and keep our code clean and modular. For this, we will register our repository and service so that they are created automatically for each request, and then we will see how controllers receive and use these dependencies.

Registering Repositories and Services in DI Container

To start with, we will first use the DI container that comes built into ASP.NET Core. All the registrations are generally done in **`Program.cs`**. So, before building the app, we will add the following lines in the configuration section:

```
builder.Services.AddDbContext<TaskDbContext>();
builder.Services.AddScoped<ITaskRepository, TaskRepository>();
builder.Services.AddScoped<ITaskService, TaskService>();
```

Now here,

- **`AddDbContext<TaskDbContext>()`** registers our EF Core context. A new context is created for each HTTP request.
- **`AddScoped<ITaskRepository, TaskRepository>()`** registers our repository.
- The **`ITaskRepository`** is the interface, and **`TaskRepository`** is the implementation. The scope means each HTTP request gets its own instance.

This registration tells ASP.NET Core how to construct and inject these classes wherever they are needed.

Injecting Dependencies into Controllers

Now, when ASP.NET Core creates a controller, it will automatically provide the needed service via the constructor, no manual setup required.

Given below is our TasksController showing it in action:

```
[ApiController]
[Route("api/[controller]")]
public class TasksController : ControllerBase
{
    private readonly ITaskService _service;
    public TasksController(ITaskService service)
    {
        _service = service;
    }
    // Now we can use _service in our actions, fully
configured and ready!
    [HttpGet]
    public async Task<IActionResult> GetTasks()
    {
        var tasks = await _service.ListTasksAsync();
        return Ok(tasks);
    }
}
```

In the above, there is no new **`TaskService(...)`** or manual wiring. Everything flows through DI, and makes the controller simple, testable, and independent of infrastructure details.

If we want to see it live, we can:

- Start the app with **`dotnet run`**.
- Make a request to **`GET /api/tasks`** using Swagger, Postman, or curl.
- The request will flow from controller → service → repository → EF Core → database, with each layer getting its dependencies from DI.

If we set a breakpoint in the controller's constructor, we will see the service is provided automatically. Each HTTP request receives a fresh context, repository, and service, keeping everything safe and isolated.

It's all about keeping Trackr's backend simple, strong, and flexible. With DI, we can add features, fix bugs, or add new layers of functionality without a hitch.

Defining API Contracts for Task Operations

We will now learn to establish a clean, professional separation between our public API and our internal data model. And this, we will do by introducing DTOs for the Task operations in Trackr. We know that the DTOs shape the data exchanged between clients and our backend, protecting our core entities from accidental leaks, future-proofing the API, and letting us evolve internal logic without breaking clients.

So here, we will build DTOs for create, update, and list operations. Then, we will see how to map DTOs to our domain entities, both when receiving data (for inserts/updates) and when returning data (for listing and details).

Defining DTOs for Task Operations

Our domain entities often contain extra fields, navigation properties, or business logic not meant for public consumption. At the same time, the API shape we expose to consumers (like frontend apps or third parties) should be stable, minimal, and clear. DTOs:

- Limit the data clients send or receive to only what is needed
- Prevent overposting and model binding security risks
- Allow us to change internal logic without forcing API updates

S, let us begin to create simple C# records or classes for each type of operation.

TaskCreateDto

This DTO is used when a client wants to create a new task.

```
public class TaskCreateDto
{
    public string Title { get; set; }
    public DateTime? DueDate { get; set; }
    public int? CategoryId { get; set; }
    public int? UserId { get; set; }
}
```

Now here, do make a note that, we do not expose fields like **`TaskId`** or **`Status`**, since those are set internally.

TaskUpdateDto

This DTO is for updating an existing task. The client may send only updatable fields.

```
public class TaskUpdateDto
{
    public string Title { get; set; }
    public DateTime? DueDate { get; set; }
    public string Status { get; set; }
    public int? CategoryId { get; set; }
    public int? UserId { get; set; }
}
```

TaskListDto / TaskDetailDto

For returning data (for listings or details), we define exactly what we want the client to see.

```
public class TaskListDto
{
    public int TaskId { get; set; }
    public string Title { get; set; }
    public string Status { get; set; }
    public DateTime? DueDate { get; set; }
    public string CategoryName { get; set; }
    public string UserName { get; set; }
}
```

This ensures consumers do not see internal IDs for related entities, but get readable names instead.

Mapping DTOs to Entities and Back

We can also map manually or use a tool like AutoMapper. For now, we will learn to use the manual approach:

From DTO to Entity (Create and Update)

```
//Create
public TaskItem MapCreateDtoToTask(TaskCreateDto dto)
```

```
{
    return new TaskItem
    {
        Title = dto.Title,
        DueDate = dto.DueDate,
        CategoryId = dto.CategoryId,
        UserId = dto.UserId,
        Status = "Pending" // Set default
    };
}

//Update
public void MapUpdateDtoToTask(TaskUpdateDto dto, TaskItem
task)
{
    task.Title = dto.Title;
    task.DueDate = dto.DueDate;
    task.Status = dto.Status;
    task.CategoryId = dto.CategoryId;
    task.UserId = dto.UserId;
}
```

From Entity to DTO (List/Detail)

```
public TaskListDto MapTaskToListDto(TaskItem task)
{
    return new TaskListDto
    {
        TaskId = task.TaskId,
        Title = task.Title,
```

```
        Status = task.Status,
        DueDate = task.DueDate,
        CategoryName = task.Category?.Name,
        UserName = task.User?.UserName
    };
}
```

Using DTOs in the Controller

In the below, we will see a controller action using DTOs:

```
[HttpPost]
public async Task<IActionResult> CreateTask([FromBody]
TaskCreateDto dto)
{
    var task = MapCreateDtoToTask(dto);
    await _service.CreateTaskAsync(task);
    var resultDto = MapTaskToListDto(task);
    return CreatedAtAction(nameof(GetTask), new { id =
task.TaskId }, resultDto);
}
```

For listing tasks:

```
[HttpGet]
public async Task<IActionResult> GetTasks()
{
    var tasks = await _service.ListTasksAsync();
    var dtos = tasks.Select(MapTaskToListDto).ToList();
    return Ok(dtos);
}
```

Practicing DTOs and mapping makes our Trackr API robust, stable, and ready for any frontend or integration, now or in the future.

Validation, Error Handling, and Logging

We will now look to improvise the Trackr backend to professional standards. And for this, we will learn to weave in three essential features, i.e ***validation***, ***centralized error handling***, and ***structured logging***. These are not just polish, they are necessary for delivering robust, maintainable, and trustworthy APIs.

Input Validation

We start by validating user input as soon as it arrives at the API, before it ever reaches our domain logic or database.

Using Data Annotations on DTOs

Here, we will enhance our DTOs with attributes so validation happens automatically:

```
using System.ComponentModel.DataAnnotations;
public class TaskCreateDto
{
    [Required]
    [StringLength(100, MinimumLength = 3)]
    public string Title { get; set; }
    public DateTime? DueDate { get; set; }
    public int? CategoryId { get; set; }
    public int? UserId { get; set; }
}
```

Now, in our controller, we can check if the input is valid:

```
[HttpPost]
public async Task<IActionResult> CreateTask([FromBody]
TaskCreateDto dto)
{
    if (!ModelState.IsValid)
        return BadRequest(ModelState);
```

// Continue with mapping and saving...

```
}
```

Custom Validation Logic

For business rules beyond data annotations, like checking that a due date is not in the past, we can write manual checks in the controller or service layer:

```
if (dto.DueDate.HasValue && dto.DueDate.Value <
DateTime.Today)
    return BadRequest("Due date cannot be in the past.");
```

Centralized Exception Handling

We do not want to repeat try-catch everywhere. ASP.NET Core lets us handle errors centrally with middleware.

We will first add exception handling middleware in **`Program.cs`**:

```
app.UseExceptionHandler("/error");
```

Next, we then add a controller to respond to errors:

```
[ApiController]
public class ErrorController : ControllerBase
{
    [Route("/error")]
    public IActionResult HandleError()
    {
        var context =
HttpContext.Features.Get<IExceptionHandlerFeature>();
        var exception = context?.Error;
        // Optionally, log the exception here
        // Return problem details for HTTP APIs
        return Problem(
            title: "An unexpected error occurred.",
            detail: exception?.Message,
```

```
            statusCode: 500);
    }
}
```

This ensures every unhandled exception returns a predictable, API-friendly error, not a stack trace or crash.

Structured Logging across API

The logging allows us to observe behavior, diagnose issues, and maintain an audit trail. The ASP.NET Core provides an **`ILogger<T>`** for every controller, service, or repository. So here, we will inject it via constructor:

```
private readonly ILogger<TasksController> _logger;
public TasksController(ITaskService service,
ILogger<TasksController> logger)
{
    _service = service;
    _logger = logger;
}
```

After this, we will then add logs for important actions and failures:

```
_logger.LogInformation("Creating new task with title:
{Title}", dto.Title);
try
{
    // Perform operation
}
catch (Exception ex)
{
    _logger.LogError(ex, "Error occurred while creating
task");
    throw;
}
```

In the above, we will:

- Use **`LogInformation`** for high-level actions.
- Use **`LogWarning`** for suspicious conditions.
- Use **`LogError`** for exceptions.

We can also inject and use **`ILogger`** in services and repositories too, for a full trace of every important operation.

Overall, by putting the above practices in place, we can make Trackr's backend robust, developer-friendly, and production-ready. It can be easily ready for real users, evolving requirements, and safe, traceable operation.

Summary

Throughout this chapter, we learned a solid and professional structure for the Trackr backend by dividing it into controller, service, and repository layers. We understood the real-world reasons for separating responsibilities, keeping web logic, business rules, and data access apart, then designed and implemented each layer step by step. In the repository, we wrapped all EF Core data operations, providing clear methods for fetching, adding, updating, and deleting tasks. The service layer handled business rules, validation, and workflow, ensuring that only correct and meaningful data entered the system. Our controllers became clean entry points for HTTP requests, delegating all logic and persistence down to the appropriate layers.

Later, we then registered each part in the DI container, ensuring that controllers received the correct service and repository instances on every request. The DTOs were introduced to separate public API contracts from internal models, preventing data leaks and enabling safer API evolution. We also practiced input validation, centralized exception handling, and applied structured logging for transparency and observability. Overall, this chapter was able to develop strong confidence and clarity for the robust backend of Trackr.

CHAPTER 10: DECOUPLED CODE WITH INTERFACES AND DEPENDENCY INJECTION

Overview

In this chapter, we will learn to build truly decoupled, maintainable code in .NET by leveraging interfaces and dependency injection. We will begin by identifying areas where the Trackr backend and optional client are too closely bound to specific implementations, which often causes friction when testing or extending the system. We will look to formalize interfaces for the repositories and business services, and then refactor classes to depend on these abstractions rather than concrete types.

Next, the chapter will teach you through advanced DI lifetimes and scopes, so we can confidently manage resource lifetimes for every part of the application, especially the EF Core context and any background services. We will gain hands-on experience creating and using fake and mock implementations, allowing us to verify the application's behavior in both successful and failure scenarios without needing a live database or external dependencies. By the end of the chapter, we will have a strong foundation for building flexible, testable, and future-ready .NET applications using the best practices of decoupled design.

Spotting Tight Coupling in Backend and Client

Before we look at real code, at first, we will clarify what tight coupling means. In a tightly coupled system, the classes or components depend directly on the details of each other's implementation, rather than on abstractions (like interfaces). If one part changes, everything connected to it is at risk of breaking. This makes code hard to test, harder to reuse, and brittle in the face of growth.

Most of the symptoms of tight coupling in a .NET project includes:

- Direct creation of classes using **`new`** in controllers or services
- Code that accesses concrete dependencies instead of interfaces
- Scattered logic that cannot be isolated or tested independently
- Difficulty swapping out components (for example, changing data storage from SQL Server to in-memory)

In the following, we will see how these issues can appear in our Trackr code.

Controllers Instantiating Concrete Classes

First, we will find the following pattern in our **`TasksController`**:

```
public class TasksController : ControllerBase
{
```

```
    private readonly TaskRepository _repository = new
TaskRepository(new TaskDbContext());

    public IActionResult GetAllTasks()
    {
        var tasks = _repository.GetAll();
        return Ok(tasks);
    }
}
```

In the above, the controller is tightly coupled to both the concrete **TaskRepository** and the **TaskDbContext**. If we want to swap the repository for a mock in a test, or change how the database is accessed, we would have to rewrite the controller. This also means our controller cannot be properly tested in isolation.

Direct Data Access in Services or Controllers

There is another common source of coupling when business logic is mixed with direct data access. For example:

```
public class TaskService
{
    public TaskItem GetTask(int id)
    {
        using (var db = new TaskDbContext())
        {
            return db.Tasks.FirstOrDefault(t => t.TaskId ==
id);
        }
    }
}
```

In the above, it makes the service completely dependent on the data access technology. If we ever want to add caching, switch to a different data source, or add pre-processing, we would have to rewrite our business logic code everywhere.

Client Code Bound to API Response Details

Now here, let us say that our Trackr client is written to parse the backend's JSON responses directly into classes that match the exact database structure:

```
public class TaskItem
{
    public int TaskId { get; set; }
    public string Title { get; set; }
    public string Status { get; set; }
    // ...other properties match database fields exactly
}
```

If the backend changes a property name or adds a new field, the client code could break, or worse, misinterpret the data. This means backend and client are tightly coupled at the data contract level.

Services That Depend on Other Concrete Services

Let us look at an example where a notification service is used:

```
public class TaskService
{
    private readonly EmailNotificationService _notifier = new
EmailNotificationService();
    public void CompleteTask(int taskId)
    {
        // Complete the task...
        _notifier.SendCompletionNotice(taskId);
    }
}
```

This code cannot be reused with a different notification system, nor can we test **`TaskService`** without also triggering real email sends. There is no abstraction between the logic and the implementation.

From all the above, we can summarize what we have found in our review:

- Controllers are bound to concrete repositories and contexts
- Services know too much about data access details
- Clients expect the backend to never change

- Cross-service calls use new-ed up concrete classes, not abstractions

In every case, the "tightness" means that a change in one place forces changes everywhere, discourages testing, and makes growth painful.

If we try to:

- Write automated tests for controllers or services
- Swap data storage or notification mechanisms
- Version our API or evolve internal models
- Move to microservices or split the backend for scaling

We will run into friction or breakages. The decoupling solves these problems by moving our dependencies onto interfaces and abstractions, using dependency injection, and shaping our API contracts to be stable and independent from internal details. In the next steps, we will systematically introduce interfaces, dependency injection, and DTOs to break these chains, making our application more maintainable, testable, and ready for future changes.

Defining Interfaces for Core Services and Repositories

The interfaces in C# declare "what" operations a class provides, but never "how." When a class depends on an interface, it is freed from the details of which specific implementation runs at runtime. This means we can substitute, test, or extend components independently.

Now in our Trackr, the most valuable places for interfaces are our business services and repositories.

Defining Repository Interfaces

We now start by extracting an interface for our Task repository.

```
public interface ITaskRepository
{
    Task<TaskItem> GetByIdAsync(int id);
    Task<List<TaskItem>> GetAllAsync();
    Task AddAsync(TaskItem task);
    Task UpdateAsync(TaskItem task);
    Task DeleteAsync(int id);
```

```
}
```

If we have repositories for categories or users, we would follow the same pattern:

```
public interface ICategoryRepository
{
    Task<Category> GetByIdAsync(int id);
    Task<List<Category>> GetAllAsync();
    Task AddAsync(Category category);
    Task UpdateAsync(Category category);
    Task DeleteAsync(int id);
}
```

Defining Service Interfaces

Next, we will create an interface for our Task service. This service encapsulates business logic and orchestrates actions using the repository interface.

```
public interface ITaskService
{
    Task<TaskItem> GetTaskAsync(int id);
    Task<List<TaskItem>> ListTasksAsync();
    Task<TaskItem> CreateTaskAsync(TaskItem task);
    Task<bool> UpdateTaskAsync(TaskItem task);
    Task<bool> DeleteTaskAsync(int id);
}
```

Similarly, if we have business logic for users or categories, those services would have interfaces too.

Refactoring Concrete Classes to Depend on Interfaces

With interfaces defined, our next task is to update the concrete classes so they depend on these interfaces, not concrete types.

Repository Implementation

The repository class implements the interface:

```
public class TaskRepository : ITaskRepository
{
    private readonly TaskDbContext _context;
    public TaskRepository(TaskDbContext context)
    {
        _context = context;
    }
    // Implement all methods from ITaskRepository...
}
```

This makes it possible to refer to the repository via **`ITaskRepository`**, not **`TaskRepository`**.

Service Implementation

Similarly, the service class should depend on the repository interface, not a concrete repository:

```
public class TaskService : ITaskService
{
    private readonly ITaskRepository _repository;
    public TaskService(ITaskRepository repository)
    {
        _repository = repository;
    }
    // Implement all methods from ITaskService...
}
```

Now, the service does not know or care whether it is getting a database-backed repository, an in-memory version, or a mock, only that it fulfills the **`ITaskRepository`** contract.

Updating Dependency Injection Registration

In our DI setup, we will register the concrete classes as their interfaces:

```
builder.Services.AddScoped<ITaskRepository, TaskRepository>();
builder.Services.AddScoped<ITaskService, TaskService>();
```

This ensures that whenever any part of the system requests **ITaskRepository** or **ITaskService**, ASP.NET Core provides the registered concrete implementation.

Refactoring Controllers and Consumers

The controllers should only depend on the service interface:

```
public class TasksController : ControllerBase
{
    private readonly ITaskService _service;
    public TasksController(ITaskService service)
    {
        _service = service;
    }
    // Actions here only call the interface...
}
```

No controller, service, or higher-level logic should "new up" a concrete implementation. Everything flows through the DI container, which creates the correct implementation and injects it for us.

By using interfaces throughout our backend:

- We can write unit tests using fake or mock implementations.
- We can add features or replace components without wide-reaching code changes.
- We have clearer contracts, making the codebase easier for new contributors or team members to understand.

Building on this foundation, the Trackr's architecture will be robust, flexible, and ready to accommodate future changes or new technologies, whether that means adding caching, swapping databases, or expanding with new services. If we want to walk through a practical test using these interfaces, or see how to extend this pattern, we are ready to keep moving forward together.

Advanced DI Lifetimes and Scopes

We will now dive deeper into DI by exploring the lifetimes and scopes available in ASP.NET Core. The application of ***transient***, ***scoped***, and ***singleton*** lifetimes will help us control how and when dependencies are created and shared throughout Trackr. This becomes especially critical for resources like the EF Core **DbContext** and any long-lived background or hosted services.

So here, in this topic, we will review each lifetime, see how to register dependencies accordingly, and assess the practical consequences for our application's correctness, performance, and stability.

Transient Lifetime

A ***transient*** service is created afresh every time it is requested. If we inject a transient service into another service or controller, each consumer gets a brand-new instance.

This is how we register it:

```
builder.Services.AddTransient<IMyFormatter, MyFormatter>();
```

Suppose we register a simple ID generator:

```
public interface IIdGenerator
{
    Guid NewId();
}
public class IdGenerator : IIdGenerator
{
    public Guid NewId() => Guid.NewGuid();
}
```

The registering with **.AddTransient<IIdGenerator, IdGenerator>()** ensures each call to **NewId()** via a resolved instance yields a unique result and no state is shared.

Scoped Lifetime

A ***scoped*** service lives as long as the current HTTP request. All dependencies injected as scoped are created once per request and shared for all objects in that request's lifetime.

This is how we register it:

```
builder.Services.AddScoped<ITaskRepository, TaskRepository>();
builder.Services.AddDbContext<TaskDbContext>(); // DbContext
is registered as scoped by default
```

When we inject **`TaskDbContext`** or **`ITaskRepository`** into controllers or services, the same instance will be used everywhere in that request. If a controller and a service both use **`TaskDbContext`**, they get the same context, so changes and tracking are consistent.

The EF Core **`DbContext`** is ***not thread safe*** and is designed for a single unit of work per request. Registering as scoped prevents cross-request contamination, and ensures all entities tracked and saved within one HTTP request share the same context.

Singleton Lifetime

A ***singleton*** service is created only once for the entire application lifetime. All components that depend on a singleton will receive the exact same instance.

This is how we register it:

```
builder.Services.AddSingleton<ICacheService,
MemoryCacheService>();
```

If we have a simple in-memory cache, we can implement and register it as a singleton. All controllers and services across all requests will use the same cache instance.

When you get DI lifetimes and scopes down, you can be sure that Trackr's backend is running smoothly, efficiently, and safely, whether it's handling fast HTTP requests or background jobs. It's all about intention when it comes to creating and managing dependencies. This gives us predictable behavior and a solid foundation for future development.

Testing with Fake and Mock Implementation

We will now learn to use ***fake*** and ***mock*** implementations of our interfaces. It allows us to simulate real dependencies, like repositories or services, without relying on the database or external systems. We can then verify that our code behaves as expected in both successful operations and when failures occur.

In the following, we will walk through creating fake and mock objects, plugging them into our service or controller logic, and writing simple but powerful tests that prove our application works correctly.

What Are Fakes and Mocks?

Fake implementations are simple, in-memory substitutes for real services or repositories. They mimic the real thing's behavior, but do not use real infrastructure.

Mocks (often built using libraries like Moq or NSubstitute) can simulate behavior, track calls, and verify that certain methods were called with expected arguments.

Both help to isolate the unit under test, making tests fast, reliable, and independent from the environment.

Creating Fake Repository

In the following, we will test our **TaskService** without talking to a real database. For this, we will start with a fake repository:

```
public class FakeTaskRepository : ITaskRepository
{
    private readonly List<TaskItem> _tasks = new();
    public Task<TaskItem> GetByIdAsync(int id) =>
        Task.FromResult(_tasks.FirstOrDefault(t => t.TaskId ==
id));
    public Task<List<TaskItem>> GetAllAsync() =>
        Task.FromResult(_tasks.ToList());
    public Task AddAsync(TaskItem task)
    {
        task.TaskId = _tasks.Count + 1;
        _tasks.Add(task);
        return Task.CompletedTask;
    }
    public Task UpdateAsync(TaskItem task)
    {
        var existing = _tasks.FirstOrDefault(t => t.TaskId ==
task.TaskId);
        if (existing != null)
        {
            existing.Title = task.Title;
            existing.Status = task.Status;
            existing.DueDate = task.DueDate;
        }
        return Task.CompletedTask;
```

```
    }
    public Task DeleteAsync(int id)
    {
        _tasks.RemoveAll(t => t.TaskId == id);
        return Task.CompletedTask;
    }
}
```

This fake keeps all tasks in memory, allowing fast and isolated tests.

Testing with Fake Repository

Now here, we will write a test for **TaskService** using the fake repository. We may think of using a test framework like xUnit or NUnit for it.

Given below is a plain C# approach:

```
public async Task TestCreateTask_Succeeds()
{
    // Arrange
    var fakeRepo = new FakeTaskRepository();
    var service = new TaskService(fakeRepo);
    var newTask = new TaskItem { Title = "Test", Status =
"Pending" };
    // Act
    var created = await service.CreateTaskAsync(newTask);
    // Assert
    var allTasks = await service.ListTasksAsync();
    if (!allTasks.Any(t => t.Title == "Test"))
        throw new Exception("Task was not created
correctly.");
}
```

We can easily run this as many times as we like, since no database is touched.

Using Mocks for Behavior Verification

For more advanced scenarios, we may try to verify that certain methods are called for example, sending notifications or logging. The mocking library like ***Moq*** is perfect for it.

Following is a quick example of using Moq:

```
var mockRepo = new Mock<ITaskRepository>();

mockRepo.Setup(r => r.GetByIdAsync(1))

        .ReturnsAsync(new TaskItem { TaskId = 1, Title =
"Test", Status = "Pending" });

var service = new TaskService(mockRepo.Object);

var result = await service.GetTaskAsync(1);

mockRepo.Verify(r => r.GetByIdAsync(1), Times.Once);
```

This will verify that the service calls the repository as expected.

Simulating Failures and Edge Cases

The mocks and fakes make it easy to simulate errors. For example, returning **`null`** from **`GetByIdAsync`** tests how our service handles missing tasks:

```
mockRepo.Setup(r =>
r.GetByIdAsync(99)).ReturnsAsync((TaskItem)null);

var result = await service.GetTaskAsync(99);

// Assert that result is null or service responds correctly
```

Or, to simulate exceptions:

```
mockRepo.Setup(r => r.AddAsync(It.IsAny<TaskItem>()))

        .ThrowsAsync(new Exception("Database error"));
```

Now, our test can verify that the service logs or returns an appropriate error.

Since we're using fake and mock implementations, we can test every service and controller in Trackr thoroughly, without needing external dependencies or manual setup. It makes sure our code works right, survives refactors, and can be trusted to behave under all conditions.

Summary

Overall, in this chapter,we figured out and dealt with the problems caused by tightly coupled code in the Trackr backend and optional client. Our first step was to take a look at how we'd put things into action. We pointed out the times when controllers, services, or clients were relying on concrete classes, which made it tough to test and improve the application. Then, we made interfaces for repositories and services more formal, changing the code so it depends on abstractions instead of implementations.

Later, we checked out dependency injection lifetime options, like transient, scoped, and singleton, and saw how they actually work in practice for EF Core DbContext and background services. At last, we figured out how to test our app using both fake and mock versions of interfaces. This let us put in place both successful operations and error conditions to see how they'd play out.

CHAPTER 11: MVVM AND WPF DESKTOP CLIENT BASICS

Overview

In this chapter, we're going to take a look at how to set up a WPF desktop client using the MVVM (Model-View-ViewModel) pattern and hook it up to the Trackr backend in a way that's easy to expand and maintain. We'll start by clearing up the architectural relationship between the desktop and the backend. We'll emphasize that the MVVM client operates as a consumer of the Web API, not as a replacement for backend logic. We'll create a new WPF project for the modern .NET platform, check out its structure, and set up the basic window for user interaction.

As we move forward, we'll be using ViewModels with property change notification and observable collections to make sure the UI stays in sync with the underlying data changes. We'll connect XAML controls to ViewModel properties using data binding, and use commands to drive actions from the interface without manual event handling. By the end of the chapter, you'll be able to connect the ViewModel to a test-friendly, in-memory service that returns data similar to the Web API so you can verify the full MVVM loop in action.

Positioning MVVM

The Trackr backend is structured around three main layers: controllers, services, and repositories. The ***service layer*** holds our business logic and orchestrates calls to the repository, which encapsulates all EF Core data operations. The API surface is defined with DTOs, providing a stable contract to any client, web, mobile, or desktop. This means all the core validation, workflow, and data integrity logic is enforced centrally, and every client simply consumes these services via HTTP endpoints.

The API exposes endpoints such as:

- **`GET /api/tasks`** to fetch all tasks
- **`POST /api/tasks`** to create a new task
- **`PUT /api/tasks/{id}`** to update a task
- **`DELETE /api/tasks/{id}`** to remove a task

All the clients interact with the API over HTTP, sending and receiving data in the agreed format.

The MVVM (Model-View-ViewModel) is a powerful pattern for WPF desktop applications, helping us organize user interfaces with clear boundaries between data, logic, and presentation. In Trackr, the ***MVVM is an approach for structuring the frontend that consumes the backend's Web API***.

We can visualize it as below:

- Backend (ASP.NET Core API)
    - Enforces business rules, validation, and persistence

    - Exposes Web API endpoints
- Client (WPF with MVVM)
    - Presents the user interface
    - Uses ViewModels to hold data and logic for views
    - Uses Models that map to API DTOs (not direct domain entities)
    - Communicates with the backend by making HTTP requests, typically through a service or API client class

So, when the user interacts with the desktop app, the ViewModel issues a request (for example, to load tasks or save a new one) via an API client. The backend processes the request, applies all its logic, and responds. The ViewModel then updates the UI accordingly.

You can simply imagine the flow when a user wants to add a task in the desktop client:

- The user enters the task details in the WPF form.
- The ViewModel collects the input and sends it as a **`TaskCreateDto`** to the backend via HTTP.
- The API validates and persists the task, returning a success response with details.
- The ViewModel updates its observable collection of tasks, and the UI refreshes to show the new entry.

This division means:

- ***All business logic stays in one place*** (the backend), reducing duplication and error.
- ***The desktop client focuses on presentation, user interaction, and smooth user experience.***

Hence, by approaching MVVM and WPF as a client of our Web API, we gain flexibility:

- We can build multiple clients (web, desktop, mobile) all sharing the same backend.
- Changes to business rules require only backend changes, with minimal impact on clients.
- The desktop app benefits from strong, tested API contracts, making development safer and more predictable.

As we move forward, our focus will be on designing ViewModels, binding UI elements in WPF, and building services that communicate with the backend API.

Creating WPF Project

We now get hands-on with building our Trackr desktop client by creating a new WPF project that targets the .NET Desktop framework. This will give us a strong foundation in the WPF project structure and help us see how the client application ties back to the Trackr domain.

Creating WPF Project

We will begin by opening ***Visual Studio*** (Community, Professional, or Enterprise edition; not VS Code, as WPF tooling is best supported in full Visual Studio).

To start with, in the start window, we first choose ***Create a new project***.

- ***Project Type:*** Select "WPF App"
- ***Framework:*** Choose ".NET 6 (Long-term support)" or newer, since .NET 9 is our backend focus.
- ***Project Name:*** Use **`Trackr.Desktop`**
- ***Location:*** Select the preferred location for source code.

Next, we then click ***Create*** to generate the project.

Running Default Window

Without making any changes, we will now build and run the project.

- Press ***F5*** or click the ***Start Debugging*** button.
- A blank window with the title "MainWindow" appears.

This default window is our canvas. We will shape this into our Trackr desktop client by adding views, viewmodels, and services that communicate with the Web API.

Connecting Project to Trackr

Now that we have the project running, we will now tie the concept back to Trackr's domain. The WPF app, using the MVVM pattern, will:

- Display lists of tasks (fetched from the backend API)
- Allow users to create, update, and delete tasks
- Reflect changes in real time, staying in sync with business rules enforced by the backend

To do this, our WPF app will need:

- ***Models***: DTO classes that match the Web API contracts (**`TaskListDto`**, **`TaskCreateDto`**, etc.)
- ***ViewModels***: Classes that manage the data, commands, and logic for each view, acting as the bridge between the UI and the backend
- ***Views***: XAML files that define how data appears and how users interact with it

At the core, the WPF client is an independent application that "talks" to Trackr's Web API over HTTP, leveraging the backend for business logic and persistence. The client remains focused on user experience, UI interactions, and seamless task management, without duplicating backend rules or direct data access.

Building Familiarity with WPF Project Structure

Before we write any code for Trackr functionality, we need to be aware of the generated project folders and files:

- The ***App.xaml*** is responsible for application-wide settings, styles, and startup.
- The ***MainWindow.xaml*** contains XAML markup for the first window the user sees. Its code-behind (MainWindow.xaml.cs) can respond to events and initialize the UI.
- New views (for example, TaskListView) and viewmodels (for example, TaskListViewModel) will be added in their respective folders as we grow the application.

Practicing with these pieces now will help us succeed when we implement MVVM, bind to backend data, and create a smooth, powerful desktop experience for Trackr.

Implementing ViewModels with INotifyPropertyChanged

We will now practice one of the foundational skills for MVVM in WPF, ***building a ViewModel with property change notification and observable collections***. For this, we will walk through creating a **TaskListViewModel** that keeps our UI in sync with backend data, and that enables live, responsive updates whenever the model changes.

Implementing TaskListViewModel

The ViewModel sits between our XAML UI and the data from the backend. It exposes properties and collections for the view to bind, and notifies the UI whenever these change. This is accomplished using the **INotifyPropertyChanged** interface.

So here, we will begin by defining a simple **TaskListViewModel**:

```
using System.Collections.ObjectModel;
using System.ComponentModel;
public class TaskListViewModel : INotifyPropertyChanged
{
    private string _statusMessage;
```

```
    public string StatusMessage
    {
        get => _statusMessage;
        set
        {
            if (_statusMessage != value)
            {
                _statusMessage = value;
                OnPropertyChanged(nameof(StatusMessage));
            }
        }
    }
    public ObservableCollection<TaskListDto> Tasks { get; } =
new ObservableCollection<TaskListDto>();
    public event PropertyChangedEventHandler PropertyChanged;
    protected void OnPropertyChanged(string propertyName)
    {
        PropertyChanged?.Invoke(this, new
PropertyChangedEventArgs(propertyName));
    }
}
```

Wiring Property Change Notifications

The key to making the ViewModel responsive is implementing **INotifyPropertyChanged**. When a property value changes, we call **OnPropertyChanged**, and any UI elements bound to that property will update automatically.

For example, if we set **StatusMessage** in our ViewModel:

```
StatusMessage = "Tasks loaded successfully.";
```

Any TextBlock in our view that binds to **StatusMessage** will instantly reflect the new value.

Exposing Observable Collections for Binding

The **ObservableCollection<T>** is designed for WPF data binding. It automatically notifies the view whenever items are added, removed, or changed, allowing our UI to stay up to date as data arrives from the backend.

So here, let us say that we want to load tasks from the Trackr Web API and display them in the UI. For this, we simply add or clear items in the **Tasks** collection:

```
Tasks.Clear();
foreach (var dto in loadedTaskDtos)
{
    Tasks.Add(dto);
}
```

If our view binds a ListView or DataGrid to the **Tasks** property, it will update as soon as the collection changes, no manual refresh required.

Connecting to View

The given below is a basic snippet of how the view might bind to our ViewModel in XAML:

```
<Window.DataContext>
    <local:TaskListViewModel />
</Window.DataContext>
<TextBlock Text="{Binding StatusMessage}" />
<ListView ItemsSource="{Binding Tasks}">
    <!-- ItemTemplate definition here -->
</ListView>
```

As the ViewModel updates the **Tasks** collection or **StatusMessage** property, the UI will reflect these changes instantly.

With **INotifyPropertyChanged** and exposing observable collections, we now have established a responsive, data-driven foundation for our WPF Trackr client. We can now very well bind the UI elements directly to our ViewModel, and any updates, whether triggered by user actions or backend responses, will appear in real time.

Data Binding and Commands in XAML

In this topic, we will now build on our MVVM foundation by wiring up ***data binding*** and ***commands*** in XAML. This step turns our ViewModel into a live interface, where users can see their tasks, interact with the data, and trigger actions like adding or completing tasks, all by connecting XAML controls to our ViewModel's properties and commands.

Binding XAML Controls to ViewModel Properties

To begin with, we will first confirm that the DataContext of our main window is set to an instance of **`TaskListViewModel`** in XAML:

```
<Window x:Class="Trackr.Desktop.MainWindow"

xmlns="http://schemas.microsoft.com/winfx/2006/xaml/presentati
on"
        xmlns:x="http://schemas.microsoft.com/winfx/2006/xaml"
        xmlns:local="clr-namespace:Trackr.Desktop"
        Title="Trackr Tasks">
    <Window.DataContext>
        <local:TaskListViewModel />
    </Window.DataContext>
    <!-- Other controls go here -->
</Window>
```

Next, we will now bind a TextBox to a property for adding a new task, and a ListView to our observable task collection in TaskListViewModel:

```
private string _newTaskTitle;
public string NewTaskTitle
{
    get => _newTaskTitle;
    set
    {
        if (_newTaskTitle != value)
```

```
        {
            _newTaskTitle = value;
            OnPropertyChanged(nameof(NewTaskTitle));
        }
    }
}
```

And in MainWindow.xaml:

```
<StackPanel>
    <TextBox Text="{Binding NewTaskTitle,
UpdateSourceTrigger=PropertyChanged}" Width="200"
Margin="0,0,0,10"/>
    <ListView ItemsSource="{Binding Tasks}" Height="200">
        <ListView.View>
            <GridView>
                <GridViewColumn Header="Title"
DisplayMemberBinding="{Binding Title}" Width="120"/>
                <GridViewColumn Header="Status"
DisplayMemberBinding="{Binding Status}" Width="80"/>
            </GridView>
        </ListView.View>
    </ListView>
    <!-- More controls for actions will be added below -->
</StackPanel>
```

Now, whenever the user types in the TextBox, the **NewTaskTitle** updates in the ViewModel. The ListView automatically refreshes it as **Tasks** changes.

Adding Commands for Actions

The commands in MVVM replace event handlers, and keeps the code out of the view and placing all logic in the ViewModel. The standard way in WPF is to use the **ICommand** interface, often implemented by a **RelayCommand** or **DelegateCommand** class.

Following is a quick **RelayCommand** Implementation:

```
using System;
using System.Windows.Input;
public class RelayCommand : ICommand
{
    private readonly Action _execute;
    private readonly Func<bool> _canExecute;
    public event EventHandler CanExecuteChanged;
    public RelayCommand(Action execute, Func<bool> canExecute
= null)
    {
        _execute = execute;
        _canExecute = canExecute;
    }
    public bool CanExecute(object parameter) => _canExecute ==
null || _canExecute();
    public void Execute(object parameter) => _execute();
    public void RaiseCanExecuteChanged() =>
CanExecuteChanged?.Invoke(this, EventArgs.Empty);
}
```

Now, we will add an **`AddTaskCommand`** in ViewModel:

```
public ICommand AddTaskCommand { get; }
public TaskListViewModel()
{
    AddTaskCommand = new RelayCommand(AddTask, CanAddTask);
}
private void AddTask()
{
    if (!string.IsNullOrWhiteSpace(NewTaskTitle))
    {
```

```
        var newTask = new TaskListDto { Title = NewTaskTitle,
Status = "Pending" };
        Tasks.Add(newTask);
        NewTaskTitle = string.Empty;
        StatusMessage = "Task added.";
    }
}
private bool CanAddTask()
{
    return !string.IsNullOrWhiteSpace(NewTaskTitle);
}
```

Finally, we will bind the Button to the Command in XAML:

```
<Button Content="Add Task" Command="{Binding AddTaskCommand}"
Width="100" Margin="0,10,0,0"/>
```

The button will automatically enable or disable based on the **`CanAddTask`** logic.

Completing Tasks with Commands

Now here, let us say that we want to allow marking tasks as complete, for this, we will define a command that operates on a selected task:

- In ViewModel:

```
private TaskListDto _selectedTask;
public TaskListDto SelectedTask
{
    get => _selectedTask;
    set
    {
        if (_selectedTask != value)
        {
            _selectedTask = value;
```

```
                OnPropertyChanged(nameof(SelectedTask));
            }
        }
    }
    public ICommand CompleteTaskCommand { get; }
    public TaskListViewModel()
    {
        CompleteTaskCommand = new RelayCommand(CompleteTask,
    CanCompleteTask);
        // Existing initialization
    }
    private void CompleteTask()
    {
        if (SelectedTask != null && SelectedTask.Status !=
    "Completed")
        {
            SelectedTask.Status = "Completed";
            StatusMessage = $"Task '{SelectedTask.Title}' marked
    as completed.";
            // Optionally, raise property changed for the item
        }
    }
    private bool CanCompleteTask()
    {
        return SelectedTask != null && SelectedTask.Status !=
    "Completed";
    }
```

- In XAML:

```
<ListView ItemsSource="{Binding Tasks}"
          SelectedItem="{Binding SelectedTask}" Height="200">
```

```
    <!-- Columns as before -->
</ListView>
<Button Content="Complete Task"
        Command="{Binding CompleteTaskCommand}"
        Width="120" Margin="10,0,0,0"/>
```

The "Complete Task" button is only enabled when a pending task is selected.

In general, when we bind properties and commands in XAML, we keep our UI and logic nice and tidy, with each part doing its own thing. All the data and behavior are in the ViewModel, and the view just reflects and triggers changes. As we move forward, these patterns will make it simple to add more complex features to Trackr's desktop client.

Showing Tasks from an In Memory Service

We will now try to make the WPF desktop client truly interactive by connecting the **TaskListViewModel** to a simple in-memory service that mimics the data structure of our Trackr Web API. This step will teach us to connect the ViewModel to a real data source, ensure our bindings work, and lay the groundwork for eventually swapping in an actual Web API client.

Building In-Memory Task Service

To start with, we will first define an interface that matches what a Web API service might offer. This helps reinforce loose coupling, and will make it easy to later switch from our in-memory service to an HTTP client.

```
using System.Collections.Generic;
using System.Threading.Tasks;
public interface ITaskDataService
{
    Task<List<TaskListDto>> GetTasksAsync();
}
```

Next, we will now create a simple implementation that stores tasks in memory:

```
public class InMemoryTaskDataService : ITaskDataService
{
    private readonly List<TaskListDto> _tasks = new()
```

```
    {
        new TaskListDto { TaskId = 1, Title = "Draft project
proposal", Status = "Pending" },
        new TaskListDto { TaskId = 2, Title = "Schedule team
meeting", Status = "Completed" },
        new TaskListDto { TaskId = 3, Title = "Review pull
requests", Status = "Pending" }
    };
    public Task<List<TaskListDto>> GetTasksAsync()
    {
        // In a real app, this would call an API
        return Task.FromResult(_tasks.ToList());
    }
}
```

Connecting ViewModel the Service

Here, we will update the **TaskListViewModel** to depend on **ITaskDataService**, and use it to load tasks.

```
public class TaskListViewModel : INotifyPropertyChanged
{
    // ...existing code...
    private readonly ITaskDataService _dataService;
    public TaskListViewModel(ITaskDataService dataService)
    {
        _dataService = dataService;
        LoadTasksCommand = new RelayCommand(async () => await
LoadTasksAsync());
    }
    public ICommand LoadTasksCommand { get; }
    private async Task LoadTasksAsync()
```

```
    {
        StatusMessage = "Loading tasks...";
        var loadedTasks = await _dataService.GetTasksAsync();
        Tasks.Clear();
        foreach (var task in loadedTasks)
        {
            Tasks.Add(task);
        }
        StatusMessage = $"Loaded {Tasks.Count} tasks.";
    }
}
```

After doing this, the ViewModel requests data from the service rather than directly from a collection or the view. This also keeps our code modular and testable.

To make the service available to the ViewModel in the running app, we need to instantiate and provide it in **MainWindow.xaml.cs**, ideally in the code-behind of the MainWindow (for small samples) or with a proper DI container in larger apps:

```
public partial class MainWindow : Window
{
    public MainWindow()
    {
        InitializeComponent();
        var dataService = new InMemoryTaskDataService();
        var viewModel = new TaskListViewModel(dataService);
        this.DataContext = viewModel;
        // Load tasks when window starts
        Loaded += async (s, e) => await
viewModel.LoadTasksCommand.Execute(null);
    }
}
```

Now, when the window opens, it triggers the command to load tasks from our in-memory service.

Because our **`InMemoryTaskDataService`** returns a list of **`TaskListDto`** items that look just like what our Web API would provide, our ViewModel and View are now ready for seamless replacement, when the time comes, we will simply swap in a real HTTP client for the service interface, and all UI binding logic will remain unchanged.

Summary

As we went through this chapter, we got the hang of the basics of creating a WPF desktop client using the MVVM pattern, which is closely tied to our Trackr backend architecture. We started by explaining how MVVM is a frontend pattern that uses Web API endpoints, and we clarified the separation of responsibilities between the desktop UI and the backend services. We set up a new WPF project, ran the default window, and mapped its purpose to our Trackr domain.

Then, we built a TaskListViewModel that notifies the UI of property changes and exposes observable collections, so the UI can update in real time. We linked controls to ViewModel properties using data binding and commands in XAML, and users can add or complete tasks through the interface. At last, we linked the ViewModel to an in-memory data service that reflected the structure of our Web API. This let us show realistic task lists, test UI logic, and get ready for smooth integration with live backend data.

CHAPTER 12: CONNECTING WPF CLIENT TO WEB API

Overview

This chapter is going to take the WPF desktop client from a local prototype to a real, connected application by setting up end-to-end communication with the Trackr Web API. First, we'll switch out the in-memory service for an HTTP-based service using **`HttpClient`**. Then, we'll take a look at serializing request DTOs to JSON and deserializing API responses into objects that are friendly for ViewModel. After that, as we add and update the tasks, we'll learn to refresh the ViewModel collections quickly, manage loading indicators for user feedback, and keep the UI in sync with the server state.

Finally, we'll try to tackle error handling, showing how to gracefully present network, timeout, and validation errors as clear, user-friendly messages. It'll feel solid, interactive, and ready for the real world by the end of the chapter. It'll show live data for every operation, and every error will be handled with care.

Switching WPF Client from In-Memory to HTTP

Up to this point, we have worked with an in-memory service that only simulated task data. Now in this topic, we will replace this with true HTTP requests using **`HttpClient`**, so that every task in the desktop app reflects what lives in our backend, no more dummy data, only live, persistent information.

We already have our **`TaskListViewModel`** using an **`ITaskDataService`** abstraction, which up until now pointed to **`InMemoryTaskDataService`**. The next step is to inject real data: when we open the desktop app, we want to see exactly what our backend knows, and every change should sync with the server.

Designing HttpClient Service for Web API Calls

We will create a new class, **`HttpTaskDataService`**, that implements **`ITaskDataService`**. This class will handle all HTTP communication with the backend. Let us break down exactly how this will work.

First, we will design the service:

```
using System.Net.Http;
using System.Net.Http.Json;
using System.Collections.Generic;
using System.Threading.Tasks;
```

```
public class HttpTaskDataService : ITaskDataService
{
    private readonly HttpClient _client;
    public HttpTaskDataService(HttpClient client)
    {
        _client = client;
    }
    public async Task<List<TaskListDto>> GetTasksAsync()
    {
        var response = await _client.GetAsync("/api/tasks");
        response.EnsureSuccessStatusCode();
        var data = await
response.Content.ReadFromJsonAsync<List<TaskListDto>>();
        return data ?? new List<TaskListDto>();
    }
}
```

From the above script,

- The service sends a GET request to **/api/tasks**.
- If the server responds successfully, it reads and deserializes the JSON array into a list of tasks.
- If the server is empty, it returns an empty list, never a null.

Configuring HttpClient and Injecting Service

Next, we need to configure the **HttpClient** so it knows where to find our backend. So for this, we will add the following in the **MainWindow.xaml.cs**:

```
public partial class MainWindow : Window
{
    public MainWindow()
    {
        InitializeComponent();
```

```
        // Set up HttpClient with backend API URL
        var client = new HttpClient
        {
            BaseAddress = new Uri("https://localhost:5001") //
Update this to match the backend
        };
        var service = new HttpTaskDataService(client);
        var vm = new TaskListViewModel(service);
        this.DataContext = vm;
        Loaded += async (s, e) => await
vm.LoadTasksCommand.Execute(null);
    }
}
```

This will ensure that when we start the app, the client talks directly to our running backend, just as a real user would.

Making ViewModel Robust against Network Issues

There are situations when we swap to real HTTP, the network errors can or may occur. So here, we want our users to always know what is happening. For this, we will update **LoadTasksAsync** in **TaskListViewModel**:

```
private async Task LoadTasksAsync()
{
    try
    {
        StatusMessage = "Contacting Trackr backend...";
        var loaded = await _dataService.GetTasksAsync();
        Tasks.Clear();
        foreach (var t in loaded)
            Tasks.Add(t);
        StatusMessage = $"Loaded {Tasks.Count} tasks from
server.";
```

```
        }
        catch (HttpRequestException ex)
        {
            StatusMessage = $"Cannot reach server: {ex.Message}";
        }
        catch (Exception ex)
        {
            StatusMessage = $"Unexpected error: {ex.Message}";
        }
    }
```

If there is a network issue or the server is offline, the users will now see a clear message instead of a broken UI.

With this, we have established a real, end-to-end connection from our desktop WPF application to the Trackr backend. All data is live, persistent, and up to date. Our desktop client is now ready to operate in a real-world environment, and every action syncs with the backend automatically. As we proceed, we will extend these same concepts for POST, PUT, and DELETE, making the Trackr desktop app a full-featured client that feels fast, reliable, and modern.

Handling Serialization and Deserialization of DTOs

We will now move on to building the fluency in moving data between WPF client and the Trackr Web API. And for this, we need to be upskilled with ***serialization*** and ***deserialization*** of DTOs. If ewe do this, we can be very sure that our requests and responses flow smoothly as JSON, and that our ViewModel always works with objects that are easy to bind and manipulate.

Serializing DTOs to JSON for Requests

When we want to send data to the API, such as adding or updating a task, we need to serialize our DTO objects into JSON. The **`System.Net.Http.Json`** namespace in .NET provides extension methods that make this process straightforward.

So here, we will add a new task. Our DTO might look like this:

```
public class TaskCreateDto
{
```

```
    public string Title { get; set; }
    public DateTime? DueDate { get; set; }
}
```

To send this as a POST request:

```
public async Task AddTaskAsync(TaskCreateDto dto)
{
    var response = await _client.PostAsJsonAsync("/api/tasks",
dto);
    response.EnsureSuccessStatusCode();
}
```

The **PostAsJsonAsync** method automatically serializes the **dto** object into JSON, sets the proper headers, and sends it to the backend.

Deserializing JSON Responses to ViewModel-Friendly Objects

When the API responds, whether with a list of tasks, a single object, or a status message, the client must turn the JSON back into C# objects, such as for retrieving all tasks:

```
public async Task<List<TaskListDto>> GetTasksAsync()
{
    var response = await _client.GetAsync("/api/tasks");
    response.EnsureSuccessStatusCode();
    var data = await
response.Content.ReadFromJsonAsync<List<TaskListDto>>();
    return data ?? new List<TaskListDto>();
}
```

If we ever need more control, we can use lower-level methods:

```
using System.Text.Json;
public async Task<TaskListDto> GetTaskByIdAsync(int id)
{
    var response = await _client.GetAsync($"/api/tasks/{id}");
```

```
    response.EnsureSuccessStatusCode();
    var json = await response.Content.ReadAsStringAsync();
    var dto = JsonSerializer.Deserialize<TaskListDto>(json);
    return dto;
}
```

Binding Deserialized Objects to ViewModel

Once we have deserialized objects, we can also simply add them to the observable collection in the ViewModel:

```
Tasks.Clear();
foreach (var task in tasksFromApi)
{
    Tasks.Add(task);
}
```

The view updates immediately, since the collection is observable and all DTO properties are ready for binding.

Handling Serialization Settings

If the DTOs use custom property names, or if we need to match backend conventions (for example, camelCase instead of PascalCase), so here, we can configure the serializer:

```
var options = new JsonSerializerOptions
{
    PropertyNamingPolicy = JsonNamingPolicy.CamelCase
};
var json = JsonSerializer.Serialize(dto, options);
```

For complex types or nested objects, we just have to ensure that all the classes are serializable and public.

Validating JSON Payloads

In the interim, you can always check what JSON will be sent by serializing and printing the string before sending:

```
string json = JsonSerializer.Serialize(dto, options);
Console.WriteLine(json);
```

This is particularly helpful for debugging API requests and making sure property names and formats match backend expectations.

Managing State and Refreshing the UI after API Calls

This topic is one of the most important aspects of a responsive WPF application. When users create, update, or delete tasks, they expect to see immediate and accurate feedback in the UI. In this topic, we will learn to update ViewModel collections as responses arrive from the server, and to manage loading indicators such that the user always knows what is happening.

Updating ViewModel Collections

When we perform an operation, such as adding, updating, or deleting a task through the API, we must refresh our ViewModel's collections to reflect the latest server state. So here, let us say that we have methods like **AddTaskAsync**, **UpdateTaskAsync**, and **DeleteTaskAsync** in our data service.

In the following, after each operation completes, we will see to update the UI:

```
public async Task AddTaskAsync(TaskCreateDto newTask)
{
    await _dataService.AddTaskAsync(newTask);
    await RefreshTasksAsync();
}
public async Task RefreshTasksAsync()
{
    var loadedTasks = await _dataService.GetTasksAsync();
    Tasks.Clear();
    foreach (var task in loadedTasks)
    {
        Tasks.Add(task);
```

```
    }
}
```

Whenever a task is added, edited, or deleted, call **RefreshTasksAsync** to pull the latest data from the backend and repopulate the observable collection. The ListView in the UI will automatically reflect these changes, as it is bound to the **Tasks** collection.

Managing Loading Indicators in UI

To provide feedback during long-running API calls, we can manage a loading flag in the ViewModel and bind it to a visual indicator in XAML as shown below:

```
private bool _isLoading;
public bool IsLoading
{
    get => _isLoading;
    set
    {
        if (_isLoading != value)
        {
            _isLoading = value;
            OnPropertyChanged(nameof(IsLoading));
        }
    }
}
public async Task RefreshTasksAsync()
{
    try
    {
        IsLoading = true;
        StatusMessage = "Loading tasks from server...";
        var loadedTasks = await _dataService.GetTasksAsync();
        Tasks.Clear();
```

```
        foreach (var task in loadedTasks)
            Tasks.Add(task);
        StatusMessage = $"Loaded {Tasks.Count} tasks from
server.";
    }
    catch (Exception ex)
    {
        StatusMessage = $"Error: {ex.Message}";
    }
    finally
    {
        IsLoading = false;
    }
}
```

And, we will update the MainWindow.xaml as below:

```
<StackPanel>
    <TextBlock Text="{Binding StatusMessage}"
Margin="0,0,0,10"/>
    <ProgressBar IsIndeterminate="True" Visibility="{Binding
IsLoading, Converter={StaticResource
BoolToVisibilityConverter}}" Height="6"/>
    <!-- ListView and other controls go here -->
</StackPanel>
```

The **ProgressBar** becomes visible whenever **IsLoading** is true. The **BoolToVisibilityConverter** is a small helper that we can define in code to translate a boolean into **Visible** or **Collapsed** for the ProgressBar.

With this, our users always see the most current data and receive clear feedback about ongoing operations, making the application feel fast, reliable, and trustworthy. This pattern holds for every API call we add, keeping our app modern and robust as it grows.

Graceful Error Handling in Desktop Client

We will now focus on one of the most important aspects of building a professional desktop client: ***graceful error handling***. In today's applications, users will encounter situations such as HTTP failures, network timeouts, and validation errors from the server. If we do not handle these conditions thoughtfully, the application can feel brittle or unfriendly. So here, we will aim to capture these failures, respond to them appropriately, and always present clear, user-friendly messages that build trust and confidence.

Handling HTTP Failures

The HTTP failures can occur for many reasons: the server might be offline, a request might be malformed, or the API might reject an action. We need to intercept these failures and update our ViewModel accordingly.

To do this, we will update the data loading logic in our TaskListViewModel:

```
public async Task RefreshTasksAsync()
{
    try
    {
        IsLoading = true;
        StatusMessage = "Loading tasks...";
        var loadedTasks = await _dataService.GetTasksAsync();
        Tasks.Clear();
        foreach (var task in loadedTasks)
            Tasks.Add(task);
        StatusMessage = $"Loaded {Tasks.Count} tasks.";
    }
    catch (HttpRequestException ex)
    {
        StatusMessage = "Cannot reach the server. Please check
the internet connection or try again later.";
    }
    catch (TaskCanceledException)
```

```
    {
        StatusMessage = "The server is taking too long to
respond. Please try again in a moment.";
    }
    catch (Exception ex)
    {
        StatusMessage = "An unexpected error occurred while
loading tasks.";
    }
    finally
    {
        IsLoading = false;
    }
}
```

By doing this, each exception is mapped to a plain-language status, and we avoid exposing raw error details to users. For example, a network failure is simply described as not being able to reach the server.

Handling Timeouts

The timeouts often happen if the server is slow or the network is congested. The **`HttpClient`** raises a **`TaskCanceledException`** when the request takes too long. We already catch this above and notify the user that the operation timed out.

However, we can also set a timeout directly on the **`HttpClient`**:

```
httpClient.Timeout = TimeSpan.FromSeconds(10);
```

This makes the app feel responsive, rather than leaving users waiting indefinitely.

Handling Validation Errors from Backend

The backend might reject requests due to validation failures, for example, missing required fields or invalid dates. The ASP.NET Core Web API usually returns a **`400 Bad Request`** status with details in the response body.

So here, we can handle this while adding a task:

```
public async Task AddTaskAsync(TaskCreateDto newTask)
{
    try
    {
        var response = await
_client.PostAsJsonAsync("/api/tasks", newTask);
        if (response.IsSuccessStatusCode)
        {
            StatusMessage = "Task added successfully.";
            await RefreshTasksAsync();
        }
        else if (response.StatusCode ==
System.Net.HttpStatusCode.BadRequest)
        {
            var errorContent = await
response.Content.ReadAsStringAsync();
            StatusMessage = $"Task not added:
{ParseValidationError(errorContent)}";
        }
        else
        {
            StatusMessage = "Failed to add the task due to a
server error.";
        }
    }
    catch (HttpRequestException)
    {
        StatusMessage = "Could not connect to the server.
Please check the network.";
    }
    catch (Exception)
```

```
    {
        StatusMessage = "An unexpected error occurred while adding the task.";
    }
}
```

We can also show the whole error message from the API, or map it to friendlier text as shown below:

```
private string ParseValidationError(string errorContent)
{
    // Simple example: just return the raw message.
    // Advanced: Parse JSON for more user-friendly details.
    return errorContent;
}
```

Disabling Actions during Errors

When loading or after an error, it's best to turn off UI actions that shouldn't be repeated. Otherwise, you might end up with confusion and more errors. So, for this:

```
<Button Content="Add Task" Command="{Binding AddTaskCommand}"
IsEnabled="{Binding IsLoading, Converter={StaticResource
InverseBoolConverter}}"/>
```

To sum up, every exception becomes an opportunity to reassure the user, keep them informed, and maintain their trust in the Trackr application. Our users will always know what happened, what to do next, and never feel lost in a sea of technical details.

Summary

All in all, we took the WPF desktop client from a local prototype to a real, connected application by setting up end-to-end communication with the Trackr Web API. We started by swapping out the in-memory service for an HTTP-based service using HttpClient, which let the client get and show live task data from the backend. Then, we focused on converting request DTOs to JSON and converting API responses into objects that are easy to work with in ViewModels. This made sure that every data exchange was predictable and reliable.

As we added and updated tasks, we learned to refresh the ViewModel collections ASAP, managed loading indicators for user feedback, and kept the UI in sync with the server state. Finally, we covered error handling, showing how to gracefully present network, timeout, and validation errors as clear, user-friendly messages.

CHAPTER 13: DEPLOYMENT, CONFIGURATION, AND MAINTENANCE

Overview

In this chapter, I'll show you how to take the web apps and the WPF desktop client from development to deployment and ongoing maintenance. I'll show to use **dotnet publish** to generate deployment packages, and we'll compare framework-dependent and self-contained outputs to choose the best approach for the scenario. Then, we'll check out to run the Web API using Kestrel, and then to securely expose it to users through IIS as a reverse proxy.

This chapter will also go over how to manage different settings for development and production environments. It'll make sure that all secrets and critical options are externalized using environment files and variables. Lastly, we'll set up solid monitoring by adding health check endpoints and organized logging. That way, we can keep an eye on the status and performance of the apps in real time. When you've got these skills, you can keep Trackr going, fix any problems, and make it better for everyone. That way, it'll always be reliable for every user and every new version.

Building and Publishing .NET 9 Applications

We will now take our Trackr Web API and WPF desktop client from development to deployment. And for this, we will learn to package and publish .NET 9 applications in this topic. In the following, we will walk through every step of producing deployable builds using the **dotnet publish** command, and we will see how to inspect both self-contained and framework-dependent outputs.

Publishing ASP.NET Core Web API

Before publishing, we need to make sure that both the Web API and WPF projects build and run correctly in the development environment. And, all the dependencies must be restored, and the code should also be free of build errors.

Publishing Web API Project

We will first navigate to the folder containing the Trackr Web API project:

```
cd C:\Projects\Trackr\Trackr.WebApi
```

We then create a framework-dependent deployment (the default mode):

```
dotnet publish -c Release -o publish
```

This above command builds the application in Release mode, and places the output in a folder called **publish** inside the project directory. In the output, you will see DLL files, the **appsettings.json**, and several dependency assemblies.

Creating Self-Contained Deployment

Now let us consider that we want to deploy to a server or user machine that does not have .NET 9 installed. So, for this, we can package everything, including the runtime, by using a self-contained deployment. We need to specify the runtime identifier (RID) for the target platform as shown below:

```
dotnet publish -c Release -r win-x64 --self-contained true -o
publish-win
```

This will build a directory called **`publish-win`** containing all dependencies, the .NET runtime, and an executable file (**`Trackr.WebApi.exe`**). It also increases the size of the output, but simplify deployment to new environments.

Publishing WPF Desktop Client

We will first change the directory to WPF project folder:

```
cd C:\Projects\Trackr\Trackr.Desktop
```

Next, to publish as framework-dependent:

```
dotnet publish -c Release -o publish
```

Here, you will see the DLLs and a config file. The users must have .NET Desktop Runtime installed.

And, to publish as self-contained:

```
dotnet publish -c Release -r win-x64 --self-contained true -o
publish-win
```

This will include **`Trackr.Desktop.exe`** and all the files required for running the app independently of any local .NET install.

When deciding which to use, I rather recommend to consider the target users. If you are looking for broadest compatibility, then you must choose self-contained, otherwise, the framework-dependent saves space and bandwidth.

With these publishing skills, we are ready to move Trackr beyond the development environment and into users' hands, whether on local servers, in the cloud, or across the organization.

Hosting Web API

Let us now walk through the process of ***hosting the Trackr Web API in a production-style environment***. We will begin by running our API behind Kestrel, the fast, cross-platform web server that ASP.NET Core apps use by default. Next, we will configure a reverse proxy using IIS (Internet Information Services), which is a common and practical pattern for deploying .NET APIs in real-world Windows server environments.

Running Web API behind Kestrel

The Kestrel serves as the internal web server for ASP.NET Core apps. It is lightweight and high-performance but is typically placed behind a reverse proxy for security, SSL termination, and management.

We will first navigate to the published Web API output directory as given below:

`C:\Projects\Trackr\Trackr.WebApi\publish-win`).

We will then start the app directly using the executable:

```
Trackr.WebApi.exe
```

Now here, by default, the Kestrel listens on the ports specified in **`appsettings.json`** or in the command-line arguments. And, the output should indicate something like:

```
info: Microsoft.Hosting.Lifetime[0]
      Now listening on: http://localhost:5000
      Application started. Press Ctrl+C to shut down.
```

The API will be now running locally, and ready to accept requests on the specified port.

Configuring IIS as Reverse Proxy

We know that the Kestrel is very secure and production-grade, but it is not designed to handle edge concerns such as HTTPS certificate management, process recycling, load balancing, or advanced logging. So, for these features, we must run the Kestrel behind a web server like IIS.

The IIS generally acts as a front-facing web server that forwards incoming HTTP requests to the Kestrel server running the application. For your information, this setup is quite common for on-premises and Windows Server deployments.

Install IIS and Required Modules

For this, we will open the ***"Turn Windows features on or off"*** and will make sure that the ***Internet Information Services*** and ***IIS Management Console*** are checked.

After this, we will then install the ***ASP.NET Core Hosting Bundle*** from the official Microsoft website. This bundle configures IIS to forward requests to Kestrel and installs the required .NET runtime.

Configure IIS Site

- Open ***IIS Manager***, right-click the ***Sites***, and then ***Add Website***.
- Next, we will set the ***Site name***, maybe "TrackrAPI", and will set the ***Physical path*** to the folder **`C:\Projects\Trackr\Trackr.WebApi\publish-win`**).
- After this, we will then set the ***Binding*** type to **`http`** or **`https`**, and will choose the ***Port*** to 80 or 8080.

Configure Reverse Proxy Handler

The ASP.NET Core Hosting Bundle installs a ***module*** (**`AspNetCoreModuleV2`**) that acts as a reverse proxy. It forwards incoming traffic from IIS to the running Kestrel process.

For this, we will check the **`web.config`** in the publish folder. It should contain an entry like the below one:

```
<system.webServer>
  <handlers>
    <add name="aspNetCore" path="*" verb="*" modules="AspNetCoreModuleV2" resourceType="Unspecified"/>
  </handlers>
  <aspNetCore processPath=".\Trackr.WebApi.exe" stdoutLogEnabled="false" stdoutLogFile=".\logs\stdout" hostingModel="inprocess"/>
</system.webServer>
```

This configuration tells IIS to start and manage the application process, and forward all incoming requests.

With the above steps, we can easily deploy and host the Trackr Web API with Kestrel and IIS, mirroring what is done in real enterprise and cloud environments. This process prepares the API for stable, secure, and scalable production operation.

Managing Environments and App Settings

We now move on to learning how to ***separate configuration from code*** in Trackr. This is necessary for our application to adapt easily to both development and production environments. This is an essential practice for scalable .NET applications, to make the maintenance simpler and reduces deployment errors.

Configuring Development and Production Settings

The most common pattern is to keep the base settings in **appsettings.json**, then override or extend them with environment-specific files like **appsettings.Development.json** or **appsettings.Production.json**.

Organizing Configuration files

Inside both the Trackr Web API and WPF projects, we will typically see:

- **appsettings.json** containing the default configuration.
- **appsettings.Development.json** includes the overrides for the Development environment.
- **appsettings.Production.json** contains the overrides for the Production environment.

For example, the **appsettings.json** might have:

```
{
  "ConnectionStrings": {
    "DefaultConnection":
"Server=localhost;Database=TrackrDb;Trusted_Connection=True;"
  },
  "Logging": {
    "LogLevel": {
      "Default": "Information"
    }
  }
}
```

While the **appsettings.Production.json** could override the connection string:

```
{
  "ConnectionStrings": {
```

```
    "DefaultConnection": "Server=prod-sql;Database=TrackrDb;User Id=produser;Password=securePwd123;"
  }
}
```

Selecting Active Environment

The .NET apps can choose their environment based on the **ASPNETCORE_ENVIRONMENT** environment variable (for Web API) or **DOTNET_ENVIRONMENT** (for desktop and non-web apps).

So, to set it on Windows for the current session:

```
$env:ASPNETCORE_ENVIRONMENT = "Development"
```

or permanently through System Properties.

Using Environment Variables

Any configuration value can also be overridden by environment variables, which are especially helpful for secrets or values that should never be stored in source control.

For example, in the API's **Program.cs**, we can read environment variables directly:

```
var builder = WebApplication.CreateBuilder(args);
builder.Configuration.AddEnvironmentVariables();
```

And, if we want to override the connection string, then:

```
$env:ConnectionStrings__DefaultConnection = "Server=prod-db;Database=Trackr;User Id=admin;Password=prodSecret!"
```

Now here, we must notice the use of double underscores (__) to represent a colon (:) in the JSON path.

Switching Settings at Runtime

When the app starts, it reads **appsettings.json** first, then overlays any environment-specific files, then finally applies any environment variables. The precedence ensures that, anything in **appsettings.Production.json** will override **appsettings.json** when the environment is set to Production. And, any environment variable will override all JSON configuration.

Next, we can also inspect the active environment in the code:

```
var env = builder.Environment.EnvironmentName;
```

And load settings or adjust logic conditionally:

```
if (builder.Environment.IsDevelopment())
{
    // Development-only services or debug configuration
}
```

Sample Implementation

Suppose we need different logging levels and database connections for development and production.

- In **`appsettings.Development.json`**, we will set:

```
{
  "Logging": {
    "LogLevel": {
      "Default": "Debug"
    }
  }
}
```

- In **`appsettings.Production.json`**, we then set:

```
{
  "Logging": {
    "LogLevel": {
      "Default": "Warning"
    }
  }
}
```

Now, on the dev machine, we will see more detailed logs, whereas in production, we will see only warnings and errors.

With this, when deploying Trackr to new environments or scaling up, we can confidently adjust settings without touching the codebase, ensuring each instance of the app is tuned precisely for its purpose.

Monitoring with Logs and Health Checks

We will now bring everything together by making Trackr production-ready and resilient, focusing on ***monitoring with health checks and rich logging***. Monitoring starts with two key building blocks: ***health checks*** for system status and ***structured logging*** for operational insight. In this, we will see to how we observe, maintain, and grow the Trackr ecosystem.

Designing and Exposing Health Checks

With health checks, we and our automated tools can check the status of our Web API whenever we want. They make sure our app is running, that it can reach its dependencies, and that core services (like the database) are healthy.

Register Health Checks in API

To do this, we will add the following in the **`Program.cs`**:

```
builder.Services.AddHealthChecks()

.AddSqlServer(builder.Configuration.GetConnectionString("Defau
ltConnection"), name: "SQL Server");
```

Post this, we can monitor the health of both our app and our SQL Server database.

Map Health Endpoint

For this, we will add the following in **`Program.cs`**:

```
app.MapHealthChecks("/health");
```

When the API runs, we will then visit **`https://yourserver/health`**. We will see a simple response:

- If all checks pass, the endpoint returns **`Healthy`**.
- If something is wrong (such as a database outage), it returns **`Unhealthy`** and an HTTP 503 status.

You can now wire this endpoint into load balancers, uptime monitors, and even deployment scripts to verify application health before routing traffic.

Integrating Rich, Structured Logging

The concept of logging is how our app talks to us in production. Without good logs, every support call becomes detective work, and root causes stay hidden. With good logs, patterns reveal themselves and diagnosis is just a matter of asking the right questions.

Setting up Logging

To start with, we will use **appsettings.json** and environment-specific files to tune the log verbosity as below:

```
"Logging": {
  "LogLevel": {
    "Default": "Information",
    "Microsoft.AspNetCore": "Warning"
  }
}
```

During development, we might want to log everything (**Debug** or **Trace**). Whereas in production, the balance between useful context and signal overload by choosing **Information** or **Warning**.

Using ILogger

Every controller, service, and background job can accept an **ILogger<T>** from dependency injection as shown below:

```
public class TasksController : ControllerBase
{
    private readonly ILogger<TasksController> _logger;
    public TasksController(ILogger<TasksController> logger)
    {
        _logger = logger;
    }
    [HttpPost]
    public IActionResult CreateTask(TaskCreateDto dto)
    {
```

```
        _logger.LogInformation("Creating new task with title
{Title}", dto.Title);

        // ... business logic ...

        _logger.LogInformation("Task '{Title}' created
successfully", dto.Title);

        return Ok();

    }

}
```

From the above, every log message can include contextual information such as user IDs, request IDs, or task titles so that tracing real-world problems is efficient and targeted.

With this, we reach the close of our journey together. We have built, debugged, refactored, tested, secured, and finally prepared Trackr for the real world. The skills we have gained here will serve not only this project, but every software endeavor we take on from now.

Summary

During this chapter, we learned how to transition Trackr from a developer's machine to a stable, production-ready system. We started by using the **`dotnet publish`** command to create both framework-dependent and self-contained deployment packages for the Web API and WPF client, ensuring that our applications could be distributed and run reliably on any target environment. We then explored how to host the Web API behind Kestrel, and how to configure IIS as a reverse proxy to provide security, scalability, and process management.

Next, we then assessed the importance of separating configuration from code, using environment-specific JSON files and environment variables to keep our settings safe, flexible, and easy to manage. We capped off the chapter, and the book, by implementing automated health check endpoints and integrating rich logging. These allowed us to monitor application status and capture meaningful operational data for diagnostics and continuous improvement. By the end of this chapter, we had fully prepared Trackr for deployment, confident that it can be maintained and observed in any environment.

Index

A

AddDbContext 157, 160, 178
ADO.NET 116, 126, 127, 128, 129, 130
Annotations 136, 166
API contracts 169, 174, 186, 187
API endpoints 16, 65, 82, 160
Authentication 117
Autos window 51, 52

B

Breakpoints 47, 50, 71

C

Collections 26, 34, 41, 188, 190, 196, 201, 207
Configuration files 220
Console I/O 19
Controllers 65, 78, 79, 80, 82, 90, 97, 101, 104, 150, 160, 171, 172, 173, 177
CRUD operations 14, 148

D

Data annotations 136
DbContext 132, 134, 140, 146, 178, 179, 183
DbSet 134, 141, 145
Debugger 47, 70
Debugging 46, 48, 61, 70, 187
Deserialization 204
DI container 95, 160, 169, 177, 198
DTO 105, 109, 162, 163, 164, 187, 204, 206

E

Entity Framework Core 15, 16, 34, 118, 131, 132, 144, 148, 150

F

Foreign keys 124

G

Generic 26, 34, 41, 196, 201
Go to Definition 10, 12, 66, 67

H

HTTP requests 65, 67, 78, 82, 85, 95, 98, 113, 150, 155, 169, 179, 186, 201, 218
HTTP responses 155
HTTP status codes 98, 110, 113, 114
HttpClient 201, 202, 203, 211, 213

I

IIS 216, 218, 219, 225
IntelliSense 10, 12
Interfaces 170, 174, 175

J

JSON configuration 221

K

Kestrel 216, 218, 219, 225

L

LINQ 19, 34, 35, 36, 37, 38, 45, 132, 141, 142, 143, 144, 148
LINQ query 143, 144
ListView 190, 191, 192, 195, 196, 208, 209
Locals window 51, 52

M

Main method 19, 20, 22, 26, 38, 45, 56, 62, 82
MapControllers 82, 84, 86, 88, 90, 98, 99, 100, 113
MapHealthChecks 223
Menu loop 26
Modules 218
MVVM pattern 187, 199

N

NuGet 4, 11, 12

O

ObservableCollection 189, 190

P

Primary keys....117
Publishing....4, 216, 217
PUT requests....108

R

Refactoring....12, 38, 73, 88, 175, 177

S

Scoped....178
Serialization....204, 206
ShowMenu....38, 39, 43, 44
Singleton....179
SQL commands....117
SQL injection....129
SQL Server Express....xvi, 2, 15, 16, 17, 115, 116, 126, 127, 130, 132, 134, 140, 141
SQL statements....132, 141

T

TaskItem class....19, 25, 31, 45, 140
TaskService....19, 40, 41, 43, 44, 45, 47, 48, 49, 50, 52, 53, 54, 55, 56, 57, 60, 61, 65, 66, 67, 68, 71, 73, 79, 80, 81, 88, 89, 90, 91, 92, 95, 153, 157, 160, 161, 172, 173, 176, 177, 180, 181, 182
Timeouts....211

U

UI binding....199
URL patterns....101, 113

V

Validation....30, 32, 105, 113, 166, 167, 211
ViewModels....185, 186, 187, 188, 213
VS Code....10, 11, 12, 13, 17, 47, 48, 49, 50, 51, 55, 61, 66, 71, 73, 187

W

Watch window....47, 51, 52, 61, 62, 72, 73
Web API controllers....98
Web API endpoints....186, 199
WPF application....204, 207
WPF MVVM....2, 15, 17
WPF project structure....187

X

XAML....185, 187, 188, 190, 191, 194, 195, 196, 199

Epilogue

We're reaching a big milestone with the adoption of .NET 9. It's got a unified platform that lets you create apps for the web, desktop, and cloud. The improvements in performance, security, and maintainability make us think bigger. Now we can design for scale, build for users we haven't even met yet, and support systems that will evolve beyond our initial vision. With each new version, .NET keeps bringing developer productivity and business-grade reliability closer together, allowing us to deliver solutions that are both innovative and dependable.

And the world of .NET development is only going to keep growing. The rise of microservices, distributed architectures, and cloud-native deployments brings both opportunities and challenges. As companies look for more flexibility and the ability to handle more work, it's more important than ever to be able to combine APIs, manage state, and deliver interfaces that respond to users' needs. The developers who can use all parts of . . . well, you know .NET, from backend APIs to rich client apps, it will be key in creating these experiences. With what you've learned here, you'll be able to contribute to projects of any size, refactor legacy code with confidence, and collaborate with teams across different disciplines and locations.

The tech world is always changing. The way we do things is always changing, but the habits of clear thinking, always learning, and solving problems well never go out of style. Now you've got the tools to move beyond tutorials and documentation, to figure out unfamiliar issues, to contribute to code reviews, and to support projects from start to finish. And with each release, new features and ideas will pop up, so being able to adapt will be your superpower. We all know that the impact of .NET 9 goes beyond the world of professional developers. With digital transformation picking up speed in all sorts of industries, there's a growing demand for software that's strong, secure, and can adapt to changing needs. The skills you've honed here can be put to use in healthcare, finance, education, and beyond. They're great at supporting both startups and big businesses, running research, and helping solve important problems. Every app you build has the power to make people's lives better, make processes more efficient, and create new opportunities for users and organizations.

As we wrap up this book, it's important to keep in mind that every project is a fresh start. You can use what you've learned as a jumping-off point, not a final destination. We'd love for you to join the .NET community, contribute to open source, share your experiences, and stay open to new ideas. You'll find the best developers are the ones who combine technical expertise with curiosity, empathy, and a willingness to experiment. The code you write today will become the legacy others inherit in the future, so build it with care and pride.

Thanks for having me, and for letting me be a part of your .NET journey. I wish you success, growth, and a deep sense of accomplishment in every line of code you create, wherever your path ends up taking. That could mean building enterprise systems, launching innovative products, or mentoring the next generation.

Thank You

www.ingramcontent.com/pod-product-compliance
Lightning Source LLC
Chambersburg PA
CBHW080211170726
48282CB00030B/1074
* 9 7 8 9 3 4 9 1 7 4 0 1 6 *